THE
SECURITY
OFFICER'S
FIELD TRAINING GUIDE

Lt. Phillip M. Satterfield, M.P.A.

THE SECURITY OFFICER'S FIELD TRAINING GUIDE

Phillip M. Satterfield
P.O. Box 447
Cypress, California 90630

ISBN 0-9616014-2-6

Disclaimer: Concepts, principles, techniques and opinions presented in this guide are provided as possible considerations. The application, use or adoption of any concepts, principles, techniques or opinions contained in this guide are the risk of the individual or organization who makes that decision. The author or his heirs shall not be held liable or responsible for any application, use or adoption of any part of this guide.

To my wife Helen for her assistance and dedication towards making this book possible. To my daughter Jody for being a valuable assistant and to my brother Jim who inspired me to complete this book.

Preface

The private security industry is one of the fastest growing businesses in the United States and Canada. It is estimated that in the United States alone, over 1.1 million security officers are employed within the field. It is reasonable to draw the conclusion that if the need were not present, the number of security officers would be greatly reduced and reliance on traditional law enforcement services would be the norm. Obviously, traditional law enforcement cannot render the level of service required or expected by individuals or corporations. Thus, private security programs are implemented to cover the specific needs for security services and fill the void.

The private security industry must then assume many roles and perform many functions. The routine business of standing facility gate control still exists in many assignments, but the other end of the spectrum involves highly complex and sophisticated security systems development and utilization. The traditional thinking that private security is limited to simple task performance has no place in our modern society. The demands being placed on the private security industry for higher employee performance brings with it the need for a better trained and competent employee who can meet these demands. The existing formal training program for security officers is, at best, limited and provides little in the way of teaching the officer how to perform his/her job assignment. This form of training is usually left to the security agency to accomplish using agency personnel and funds. It is also rare that an organization requiring security services would pay additional funds to a security agency to train employees for the job. It is usually expected that security officers given an assignment will already have the abilities and training to perform the required task.

While the above relates more to individuals or organizations who utilize "non-employee" security services, the organization that has a security program consisting of employees recruited and trained by them seldom has the availability of funds to expend on programs that require extensive training. While security services are necessary, they are also expensive and are not, as a rule, able to equate to a profit producing part of the organization. It is, therefore, absolutely necessary that security personnel have the ability and training to perform the assignments given in a professional and competent manner.

This field training guide was designed with two main goals which are expressed throughout. The first goal is to assist the security officer in performing his/her assigned duties with confidence and increased job knowledge. The second goal is to assist the security agency that employs and supervises security officers by providing a resource their security staff can utilize in the training of their employees.

The catalyst for writing this guide resulted after publishing two books directed at preparing police recruits for entry into the law enforcement training program. It was from my years as a police academy training advisor and research into writing these books that I realized a training guide for security officers would be of value to both the individual security officer and the security agency. The benefit to the agency is seen in less training cost required for each officer. The officer will benefit by having a training guide that is directed at his/her specific needs and can be used as a reference.

In this guide I attempted to address as many circumstances and situations as possible that the security officer may face under realistic conditions. I do not assume to cover all possible conditions and assignments a security officer may encounter. However, I did attempt to look at the performance of a security officer from a practical approach and incorporate suggestions and opinions which may make the job easier to perform.

If I have been able to make the individual security officer more informed and knowledgeable about his/her delivery of professional security services, then I have accomplished my goals.

Phillip M. Satterfield, M.P.A.
Police Lieutenant
Cypress Police Department
Orange County, California
            And
Executive Training Advisor
Criminal Justice Training Center
Golden West College
Huntington Beach, California

Contents

Introduction

This Field Training Guide is intended to supplement other forms of training the security officer has completed. The broad spectrum of services the security industry provides makes it impossible to present every subject or situation that may be encountered. Some tasks are performed so infrequently that little value would be gained in detailing techniques on how to handle these situations.

Two criteria were used in selecting topics for discussion. The first criteria is the number of security personnel who perform the task, and the second is the frequency with which these tasks are performed. The majority of security officers will, at one time or another, provide security for commercial complexes. Therefore, it makes sense to discuss techniques in foot patrol or vehicle patrol of these structures. The average security officer will not be involved in providing security at bomb disposal sites, so a discussion on handling explosive devices would be of limited value.

This guide was designed to provide the individual security officer with the knowledge to perform tasks as a generalist, not a specialist. Specialization in one or more fields requires a considerable amount of training, both formal and on-the-job to reach the level of an expert. This is not the goal of this guide. The generalist security officer is one who can perform the majority of assignments with a level of competency that satisfies any reasonable expectation an employer could impose. The generalist is also the most flexible officer an agency could employ. He/she can be used in all kinds of positions with the ability to perform minor to complex assignments.

It should be understood that any book represents the opinions and recommendations from one source. Many opinions exist from various sources as to what constitutes the best way to perform a task. No single source will always offer the ideal solution to a problem. The officer must take information from all available resources and apply this data to the situation found on the job. Some techniques will offer the best way to perform a task at one time but not another. The officer will have to adapt techniques to situations in order to find the ideal solution.

This guide is written in a manner that allows easy understanding. It includes not only recommendations, but in many cases, also the rationale behind the technique proposed. Examples are used when they will help the officer to understand the concepts being presented. This guide was intended to be different from other guides that may be available to the security officer. It is written by a police officer who has 18 years of on-the-job experience and 10 years of experience in training police officers to perform their job in a safe and competent manner. Under my supervision as a Police Academy Executive Training Advisor, thousands of police recruits have been trained to perform tasks that range from routine to high risk. This experience and training is incorporated into this guide with the specific intent of assisting the security officer to be as knowledgeable and competent as possible. It is this author's sincere hope that this book will prove to be a valuable resource and become part of the officer's most reliable references.

Read this guide and carry it with you while performing the job. It will prove to be a valuable resource that offers practical alternatives and recommendations that will benefit both you, the security officer, and the agency that employs you. If this guide does what it is intended to do, then the security officer will be one who is reliable and a company asset. GOOD LUCK!

CHAPTER ONE

Employment Considerations

Employment Considerations

There are several factors that must be taken into consideration when employment within the security field has been obtained. The majority of these considerations are applicable to any profession, while some are directly related to the security industry. What can be derived from these considerations is a common sense approach that most individuals know but frequently forget. In reading this section, keep in mind that needs of the individual and the organization that acts as employer are not only related, but are so similar as to make them almost a single need. This section also centers around relationships that are both personal and professional.

EMPLOYER/EMPLOYEE RELATIONSHIP

A common bond and implied relationship exists between the employer and employee in any employment agreement. The employee agrees to provide his/her services for compensation. The employer agrees to provide compensation for services rendered. Both parties benefit from this relationship, in that each receives a return on their investment. One will not benefit without participation on the part of the other. This statement is simple in nature but is also very true. Difficulty arises when one party does not keep their part of the agreement. The employer does not benefit unless the employee provides the services required. The employee does not retain the benefit of continued employment unless he/she does a competent job. It's not difficult to understand the mutual rewards received when both parties are working towards the same goals. After all, the goals in this relationship are identical, since profit and continued employment are the motivational factors.

One of the best ways to foster a good working relationship between the employer and employee is to have open lines of communication. This doesn't mean that communication is from the top down, but it should be from both directions. The organizational management must establish policy and procedures employees know and comply with. This form of communication is absolutely necessary and no organization can be effective and continue to exist without it. The employee having these standards of job performance applies them to the job assignment and with little variance, has no difficulty working within these boundaries. While performing the job an employee may find a better and more effective way of doing the task assigned which may vary from the stated policy and procedures. At this point, effective lines of communication may not only prove valuable to the organization but also toward a positive employer/employee relationship. The employee, in transmitting this information to the decision making authority, has in no way detracted from the organizational effectiveness but has greatly enhanced it. If the decision is reached to implement the suggested change, the results can prove to be a smoother operating organization. Even if the suggestion is viewed as being an excellent idea, but for economic restraints or other factors it cannot be implemented, the exchange of ideas and open communication has more of a positive impact on organizational relationships than may be realized.

In this discussion, an attempt was made to offer the concept of employment bonding. It is from this bonding that both the individual and organization have the opportunity to expand and achieve common goals. When the employee has the opportunity to participate in the decision making process it should be utilized to the fullest. The employer who encourages employee participation has much more than an employee working for the organization, but an employee who is interested in the development and success of the organization. This employee has more value than five less motivated employees.

EMPLOYEE ATTITUDE

This topic may generate questions as to its relationship to employment considerations. Attitude is just as important to employment as is job performance. Attitude is often misunderstood or never considered an important part of the employment relationship. In many respects, attitude can be seen as an indicator of the individual's capabilities and willingness to direct his/her best efforts towards doing a good job. It's difficult to argue with the concept that an employee with a negative attitude would have difficulty performing job tasks at maximum proficiency. It seems that everyone has, at one time or another, worked with an individual who displays a poor attitude about everything, including the job. This individual not only is difficult to work around, but soon begins to have a negative effect on other employees. This individual will not only remain stagnant, as far as promotions are concerned, but will probably be unemployed very soon.

From the employer's viewpoint, while security services are necessary, they are not a profit producing asset. While it is agreed that an effective security program will allow for profit to be made by prevention of thefts and property damage, it still is not the direct source of profit. It is an expense individuals or corporations are willing to pay, as long as the service meets or exceeds the expectations. It is important to remember that these expectations may not always be security related. The overall effective operation of the organization can be a major consideration. This concept relates to attitude when attitude has a negative impact on other employees. If an attitude problem exists which begins to alter or effect other employee's productivity, it only makes sense to remove the problem.

Now that the negative aspects of attitude have been discussed, a look at the aspects of a positive attitude on the organization needs equal treatment. As stated above, everyone has worked with people who display a negative attitude. It's also true that most people have worked with co-workers who have an excellent attitude, not only about the job, but also about themselves. There is no question about which employee is more enjoyable to work and be associated with. They have the ability to make the work place an environment that produces a better product and at the same time fosters a pleasant and healthy atmosphere in which to work.

Several scientific studies have been done on the work environment in order to see the impact on performance of employees under varied circumstances. These studies have usually related to the management/worker environment in an attempt to produce a better output combined with better employee satisfaction. It would be interesting to see the results of a major scientific study on the impact of a single negative employee on an organization's effectiveness. It wouldn't be a surprise to find that just one negative employee could have a serious effect on the ability of the organization to achieve its goals and objectives. This study would have even greater impact if that employee was a manager or supervisor who had wide ranging influence over the entire organization.

EMPLOYEE MOTIVATION

The employee who possesses a high degree of motivation is not difficult to locate within any organization. This employee has developed those traits and qualities that employers view as valuable assets. Individuals may express motivation in various ways but many common factors are present and can be identified. It is common to find that motivated employees are those that receive many of the benefits the organization has to offer. Advancement, selection for special assignments, premium salary, and continued employment are only a few of the benefits that can be received.

The reason motivated employees receive first consideration is not difficult to understand when the employer's point of view is considered. An employer wants employees that have the ability to do the job they are hired to perform. They want the best person they can find who has the ability to learn job task with the least amount of training and supervision. This results in less training cost and minimal follow-up monitoring. The motivated employee not only meets these requirements, but exceeds them in all respects. The motivated employee has the ability to learn the job task not only because he/she has to, but because they want to. They require less supervision because they have the work ethic of providing an honest day's work without having to be closely supervised. This allows the employer to fulfill job requirements with the least expenditure of funds and manpower. The employer is not the only beneficiary of being able to provide a product at a minimum cost. The employee benefits when funds are made available for salary increases, equipment purchases and advancement. The result is a mutual benefit being shared by both the employer and employee.

The motivated employee often looks at the job with much more enthusiasm than one who is only profit motivated. Profit may satisfy the basic needs of the individual, but seldom satisfies the emotional needs. The desire to do a good job, reach goals and objectives, develop expertise in a given field and to satisfy the need for self-worth all serve to fulfill emotional needs with little relationship to profit. Granted, profit motivation must be satisfied before any emotional needs are to be addressed. Once this is accomplished, profit often becomes a secondary consideration.

One important trait the motivated employee demonstrates is the ability to report for duty on-time, unless ill or circumstances exist that are beyond his/her control. To the motivated employee, this is not difficult to accomplish. To others, it is almost impossible. The problems an employer must face when personnel assigned to work fail to show up on time can be very costly. It may require on-duty personnel to remain on the job at an overtime rate. It may also be necessary to assign supervisory personnel to cover the position until the officer finally arrives. This removes the supervisor from his/her duties, which equates to a loss of manpower for unnecessary reasons. It is important to understand what "on-time" really means. It does not mean that the security officer arrives at the work place prior to the scheduled work time. The officer may arrive prior to the required time, but may not be prepared to start the job. A prime example is when the officer arrives fifteen minutes prior to beginning his/her shift, but requires thirty minutes to dress and take care of other personal business. His/her physical presence is on-time, but in reality, the officer is fifteen minutes late for work. When several officers have the same trait, it's easy to understand how the problem becomes compounded and very costly.

One of the most important traits a motivated employee displays is the willingness to function as a team worker. The individual security officer may work single-officer assignments, but does not forget that he/she is part of a team. The officer knows that his/her conduct and job performance is a reflection on the entire organization, and for that matter, on the entire profession. This willingness to function as a team worker is a valuable trait that is seldom overlooked by supervision. A team worker also has little difficulty in acting as a trainer of other security officers who have less experience. He/she will also take the opportunity to offer suggestions that may be a cost savings, or make the job easier to accomplish. In many respects, a team worker is more valuable than several officers who work independent of the organization.

A security officer's appearance can be a direct reflection on his/her level of motivation. It takes time and energy to ensure that a professional image is being projected. A neat, clean and properly tailored uniform can soon be reduced to an unkempt condition without motivation. Personal hygiene and weight control are two other factors that have a direct reflection on the officer's desire to maintain a professional appearance. A person who takes little pride in his appearance, whether it's on or off the job, soon dedicates less and less time towards appearance. The officer who maintains a positive appearance will soon realize that benefits derived far exceed the time spent. The officer who cares about appearance will take the time and patience to accomplish the following preparation steps:

1. Uniform shoes will be shined to a high gloss.
2. Uniforms will be tailored and neatly pressed.
3. The officer will have neatly trimmed hair that projects a positive image of the agency and profession.
4. Moustaches and sideburns will be neatly trimmed.
5. Weight control will be maintained to acceptable health and agency standards.

6. Equipment worn will be polished and neat in appearance.
7. Personal hygiene will be maintained to prevent an unkempt appearance.
8. Posture will be such that a professional image is being projected.

CUSTOMER RELATIONS

The most successful security officer is one who has social skills which enable him to effectively deal with all segments of society. These skills include the ability to treat everyone, regardless of their nationality, religious beliefs, economic status or gender, in a professional manner. To express any form of bias can make the officer ineffective as an employee or professional security officer. It is in the best interest of the officer to practice a style of conduct which does not show preference, for or against, any individual or group.

If the officer would keep one important fact in mind, complaints or allegations of misconduct would be greatly reduced: "Treat people the way you would want to be treated." This simple statement has such an impact on the officer's ability to do an effective job, it should be the title for a separate book and required reading by everyone. If the officer would reflect back on a situation where he/she was treated by someone in a manner that was considered unacceptable, this concept would need no additional discussion. What happens is that the officer forgets to use his/her own good judgement when switching from customer to security officer. Granted, the role of security officer has a certain amount of authority; and this authority can be abused, or used in a positive manner. Those who abuse authority, will soon find employment difficult to retain. No one will accept abusive treatment, in an official or unofficial capacity.

Security officers must foster positive customer relations if they expect to do their job effectively. Positive customer relations are accomplished in many ways, not in the least by being friendly, courteous, unafraid to smile, speaking in a non-authoritarian manner and by assisting rather than ordering.

Officers will find cooperation, more often than not, when the proper mannerisms are used in performing their job. One excellent way to prove how effective a friendly approach can be is to monitor how much cooperation is given by those people who feel the officer was helping them, not abusing them. The officer will find that not only will the individual cooperate, but will often become one of the best supporters of the security program. This will serve to show that a supporting approach is much better than one that is authoritative.

The security officer will have contact with most segments of society. Some will accept whatever treatment they receive, though not liking the negative treatment, without comment or complaint. Some people will take a friendly contact and retell it in a negative way. This may be due to being told what to do, no matter how justified or friendly the request was made. These situations cannot be avoided but can be overcome by the officer's reputation for being fair and impartial in performing the job. The officer's reputation can go a long way in refuting false complaints of misconduct. The officer who consistently conducts himself in a manner that is without bias or misuse of authority will build a positive reputation by action rather than by desire. The officer needs to be consistant in performing the job, not just during certain situations, but at all times. After all, reputations are based on a lengthy pattern of behavior not on a single incident. It takes time and patience to prove that character and maturity are the officer's true traits, not just a false impression the officer wants to portray.

The security officer must look at everyone he/she comes in contact with as a customer. They may only be observed or contacted once, but the reality is that they could have an impact on the officer's career. Treating people in a fair and respectful manner can only lead to mutual understanding and development of a positive relationship. Treating people in a negative manner can only lead to mistrust and resentment. The officer wants to be effective and do the best job possible. This is accomplished by projecting the image of a professional, not as one who needs to be abrasive in order to be effective.

PROFESSIONAL CONDUCT

The professional security officer is one that adhears to a universal code that governs his/her conduct. The terms "Code of Ethics", or "Code of Conduct" have been used to describe this concept but regardless of terms used, they all relate to how the security officer conducts himself, both on and off the job. Most professionals have standards that each member of that profession agrees to uphold. While sanctions for violating these codes can vary from organization to organization, it is only important to remember that violations will be subject to discipline. In addition to formal codes of conduct, most employers will have similar standards contained in employee rules and regulations.

Professional conduct can better be explained when what constitutes unprofessional conduct is examined. Unprofessional conduct for a doctor may be issuing unnecessary prescriptions. An attorney may show unprofessional conduct by representing false documents as originals, knowing they are false. A police officer may enforce the law on some groups and not on others. As you can see from these examples, unprofessional conduct can be related to violations of the accepted behavior on the part of each professional.

Professional conduct for the security officer is not that different from any professional code of conduct standards. Professional conduct means the officer will not subject him or his profession to any undue embarrassment, demeaning criticism or unfavorable image, within or without the profession. This means that the officer will not violate any laws or established rules and regulations the employer has determined as acceptable conduct. In many cases, this can be reduced to the "an honest days work for an honest days pay" work ethic.

It would be easy to provide a list of crimes which if violated would constitute unprofessional conduct. This is frequently done to illustrate this concept. A list of this type does not satisfy the necessity to understand what constitutes professional conduct. Professional conduct means much more than just being a good citizen or employee. It involves the officer's total approach to being a security officer. How he/she views the job, what he/she does to make it a professional organization, what knowledge and dedication he/she brings to the job and the genuine desire to better him/herself through experience and superior job performance; all of these characteristics represent integral parts of professionalism. Professionalism is not easy to accomplish! If it were, then anyone could be a professonal and the term professional would have little meaning.

In order to be a professional, you must have the strong desire to want professional status, then conduct yourself in a manner that shows this desire is not just represented by empty words, but supported by actions. It's not at all difficult to be unprofessional, what is difficult is to maintain professional conduct standards that last an entire career.

CHAPTER TWO

Interview
Techniques

Interview Techniques

There are four basic types of interviews a security officer will conduct. They consist of interviews with victims, witnesses, informants and suspects. The goal to achieve in any interview situation is to obtain information that will allow you to document an accurate accounting of an incident or event. In order to accomplish this goal, information must be obtained that will answer the major elements of any report: what occured, when did it occur, where did it occur, how did it occur, why did it occur and who was involved or committed the incident. This information satisfies the who, what, when, where, why and how elements of a complete reporting process.

When interviewing in any of the above categories, it is important to remember that each may have information concerning an event or incident, but may have perceptions of what occurred from differing points of view. The victim may be emotionally upset and provide information that is not based on fact but opinion and emotional reaction. A witness may also have information but may not have witnessed the entire event. The information provided may not be complete and may only provide partial data. This situation can be compounded when the witness is related or is a friend of the victim. Emotional involvement with the incident can also influence the perception of what was observed.

Informants, as referred to in this discussion, are those individuals who have information concerning an incident that is not influenced by relationship or involvement. This differs from the traditional view of an informant being one who works undercover to gather information. The reality is that when an informant operates in an undercover capacity they are witnesses, not informants. Information received from informants can be looked at as rather reliable, as long as this information is not based on involvement. The reason for providing information may also have an impact on its validity. An informant may not be involved in an incident, but may not like an individual or group that is involved. This situation may make apparently non-influenced information biased or vindictive. The previous reasons make it necessary to uncover the motivation behind the informant's disclosure of information and take care in verification of accuracy.

Suspects provide information that requires the greatest amount of verification. The suspect who appears cooperative and admits involvement in an incident may, in fact, be providing accurate information. The opposite end of the spectrum may also be true. The suspect may admit involvement but to a lesser degree than reality. They may attempt to provide justification for acts that would appear to make them legitimate, and they may say that they did not think the act was illegal. Suspects may sometimes, if not frequently, deny involvement and provide little or no information at all. In cases like this, the security officer may have to rely solely on information obtained from other categories or from evidence obtained at the scene of the incident or event.

Now that a general overview of each interview type has been provided, a look at some specific approaches and techniques to consider when interviewing can make this process more successful. It is important to remember that any interview, regardless of the individual's involvement, requires a calm and professional approach. In the section on general considerations for conducting interviews, the interviewer's role and demeanor will be presented and will apply to any interview situation.

VICTIM INTERVIEWS

Interviewing of victims can run from highly emotional to unconcerned, depending upon the victim's state of mind during the interview. Victims who have suffered a personal loss or injury can be the most difficult to interview. They may be so upset that rational thought may not be possible. Should this condition exist, it may be better to suspend the interview until the victim is calm enough to provide accurate and factual information.

When information is absolutely necessary and must be obtained regardless of the victim's condition, a few techniques can be employed that may enhance the opportunity for a successful conclusion. One immediate consideration is to have a friend or relative remain with the victim in order to assist in calming the situation. Remember to remain calm during your questioning so that emotions are stable and do not fluctuate. Try to conduct the interview in surroundings that are familiar to the victim. The residence or work place of the victim may offer the ideal location. The main point to remember is that the interview location should be private and free from interruption. It may be necessary to allow the victim to describe the incident in his/her own words, which may include a lot of information that is not relevant. This can have a calming effect and allow for the venting of frustrations. It is important to allow the victim to complete the story before you begin to ask questions that narrow the information to more specific facts. Be considerate of the victim's physical needs by allowing him/her to make restroom visits and acquire food and drink if needed.

Victims may withhold information that could be embarrassing or make them appear incompetent. The victim who forgets to lock and secure their vehicle or desk, may be emphatic about having done so in order to show their attention to detail. One of the most frequent examples of this is when a victim reports a theft of property, when in reality, the victim lost it. The theft report is used to save face, or transfer the blame to a nonexistent theft. Proving a theft did not occur may never be possible, however, knowledge that individuals may use this tactic can help evaluate the circumstances, especially when the physical evidence does not support the allegation.

Victims have the potential to overexaggerate the loss or injury. It is common to find that the victim has greatly increased the amount of loss for insurance purposes. This also holds true on reporting an assault and battery or other personal injury. Enhanced accountings of the amount of injury serve to bolster the victim's injury and show that the suspect is deserving of prosecution. Reports of the loss or injury can also serve to support civil lawsuits against individuals or organizations. In cases of this nature, the security officer is being used as a tool to secure a favorable lawsuit verdict.

It is possible that the conditions discussed above may never be encountered. Victims reporting loss or injury may be reporting legitimate incidents. The loss or injury did occur just as reported with no variations or withholding of information. These reports and subsequent interviews offer no difficulty in documenting or taking appropriate action. A problem exists when information provided by a victim, or anyone for that matter, is received as accurate and factual without attempts at verification.

WITNESS INTERVIEWS

Interviewing witnesses can be the most valuable source of information. Most witnesses are uninvolved with the incident and will provide information that is not biased or influenced. It is important to remember that witnesses, and for that matter anyone with information, should be contacted and interviewed as soon as possible. The uninvolved witness can forget valuable information when there is a lengthy time lapse between the incident and interview.

The witness should be allowed the opportunity to completely tell the story before the officer stops them with questions for detail refinement. Remember, a witness has the information developed in his/her mind, as well as the sequence used to describe the incident. If the officer stops them during their thought process, the details may be forgotten that would otherwise have been provided. Once the story has been completed, it is acceptable, at that time, to go over the information. The tendency is to want immediate clarification on points the witness makes. This can cause the witness to become confused and lose their train-of-thought.

As previously mentioned, a great deal of information a witness provides will have absolutely no bearing on the case. It then becomes necessary to separate relevant data from opinions and nonrelated information. This technique is enhanced with experience at interviewing and it takes time to develop.

A witness to an incident will frequently have valuable information but be reluctant to become involved for a variety of reasons. The suspect may be a friend or relative, the possibility that peers may look upon the witness as a "snitch" or the fact that court testimony may be required, all serve as a deterrent to being a witness. It is difficult to overcome these problems based on the fact that any or all may exist or take place in the future. If a witness, for example, asks if he/she will have to testify in court, the witness should be advised that testimony may be necessary. It is important to address the concerns a witness may have, but not to the point he/she would decline involvement. If these issues present themselves, the best way to resolve them is by honest answers.

Often witness reluctance is based on a lack of knowledge of the criminal justice system process. If explained in the correct manner, then apprehensions can be avoided or at least suppressed. Advise the witness that information obtained will be made part of an official report, the future of which depends upon police and court action. It is not a highly recommended tactic, but a reluctant witness can be subject to subpoena in court, even as an unwilling witness, and failure to testify will be a contempt issue. The reason this tactic is not recommended is that it can be taken as a threat by the witness and may make it a challenge not to cooperate.

A professional approach to witness interviews is the best method of soliciting needed information. The interviewer who conducts the interview in a businesslike manner, without drama or use of little known legal phrases and terms, will find that most interviews will be successful. One of the quickest ways to cause a witness not to cooperate is the overbearing demeanor of the interviewer. A gruff and demeaning attitude will be received in a negative manner. The person interviewed can become angry at this form of treatment and provide information of little or no value. This is not due to a lack of information, but due to the lack of social skills the interviewer has displayed. The interviewer who shows understanding and concern for the witnesses will be the most successful.

Granted, the normal witness interview will be uneventful and consist of a normal exchange of information. Witnesses will come forth without reluctance or hesitation. This is the ideal situation and, hopefully, the previously mentioned problems will never be encountered. When they do, be professional and businesslike in your approach, keeping in mind that not all witnesses will cooperate and not all will be uncooperative.

INFORMANT INTERVIEWS

Informants can be an excellent source of information. Of the four major interview categories, informants offer the least amount of difficulty in interviewing. The informant usually comes forth on their own to give information which eliminates the reluctance problem witnesses may pose. Informant information can also pass the test of reliability when information provided is found to be unbiased. Informants who have provided reliable information in the past can also be shown to have established credibility. Credibility is an important factor when use of informant information is contested at a later date.

Several factors should be considered when informants are interviewed. The primary factor to look at is the motivation behind the informant providing the information. It is common to find that reward, praise, dislike for the suspect and being a good citizen are reasons that motivate an informant. Keep in mind, the stated reason may not be the actual reason. An informant may present himself as a concerned citizen, while the actual motivation is reward.

Often interviewers are reluctant to ask an informant why they come forth with information. There is nothing wrong with asking this question, as long as it is asked at the right time. The right time is usually at the conclusion of the interview, not at the beginning. The informant who is asked why they are providing information at the start of the interview may be embarrassed or take the question as a form of insult. Be careful to ask the question in a manner that does not offend the informant. One way to pose a question of this type is to refer to a third party, "My supervisor will need to know what, if any, relationship you have to the case, and why you are providing this information." In posing the question in this manner, you are not the one who is interested in the answer; your supervisor is. This may release the tension on the part of the informant and at least allow your rapport with him/her to continue.

Information provided by informants can be considered hearsay, which requires supporting evidence to be valid. An example of this form of hearsay would be the informant telling the interviewer that the "rumor" is a certain person committed a crime. This alone would not withstand any test of reliability unless other evidence is found to support this "rumor." This information can certainly be used to focus the investigation towards the named individual, but not as direct evidence such as fingerprints or eyewitness testimony.

Information provided by informants requires the greatest amount of verification. It is absolutely necessary that interviews with informants be as detailed as possible, focusing on accuracy and content. Taking what an informant says at face value is a risk that should be avoided. Remember, the interviewer in some cases is only a documentor of information. If the information is found to be of little value to the case, then subsequent use is limited. Informant's information usually is directly related to the case and is of considerable value. Using this information for case preparation or followup investigation can often mean success or failure in the final analysis. Solicit information from informants with the view that the value of the information can depend on the ability to verify its contents.

SUSPECT INTERVIEWS

Interviewing suspects offers the greatest challenge for an interviewer. Suspects can range from totally uncooperative to totally cooperative with many increments in between. The uncooperative suspect may refuse to communicate with you to the extent of walking out of the interview. The cooperative suspect may not only provide information on the case in question, but may admit guilt to unreported crimes. The truth of the matter is that some suspects will admit to being guilty to release their tension and guilt feelings. It is also true that some suspect's won't even admit to being alive much less to committing a crime.

Interviewing suspects requires the interviewer to maintain the highest level of control over the interview. Suspects can try avoiding the issue with unrelated stories and useless data. The interviewer should ask specific questions that require specific answers. Questions such as: "What do you think?" or "Is it possible?", only lead to vague answers or a nonspecific response. Questions such as: "Did you?", are hard to avoid or get around. Interviewers should use relevant questions that pertain to a specific case. The question, "Have you ever committed a crime?", may be specific but not relevant. The question, "Did you take money from the office cash box last night?", is both specific and relevant.

Usually, suspects are the last individuals to be interviewed. Victims, witnesses or informants have been interviewed to obtain all the facts and evidence that is available. If sufficient information exists to support prosecution, even though prosecution may not have been intended, what the suspect does or does not admit may have little bearing on the outcome of the case. A case concerning employee thefts can serve as an excellent example of this concept. A store clerk is observed by another employee removing cash from the register for no legitimate reason, and places it in her purse. Management is notified and the security department begins to monitor the transactions made by that employee. The employee is observed taking cash from a customer without ringing up the sale. The clerk places the money in her purse, instead of the register. Security, monitoring the clerk, contacts the customer to find out that a purchase was made and no receipt was given. The security officer also finds out that the customer paid for the merchandise with exact change, thus, eliminating the need to open the register. With this information, the clerk is confronted and denies any theft. In the above scenario, sufficient evidence exists to support prosecution, if desired, along with disciplinary action on the part of the company. The suspect's denial did not override the facts and evidence and, in fact, had little impact on proving the suspect had committed a crime. The suspect may eventually admit guilt, once the evidence obtained against her is presented. This frequently occurs when the suspect realizes that an overwhelming amount of evidence exists.

It may not be necessary nor practical to record interviews with all victims, witnesses and informants. If possible, it is advisable to tape record suspect interviews. This will prevent the suspect from denying they made certain statements at later disciplinary processes. Admission of guilt by a suspect can easily be denied but when the admission is recorded, it becomes very difficult to refute. A recording cannot take the place of a good report, it can only act as supporting evidence.

In interviewing a suspect, do not make the mistake of "making deals" to solicit his/her cooperation. This tactic can make a confession invalid due to promises of lenient discipline or of no official action to be taken. The suspect has an automatic defense to any admission of guilt by stating it was given to avoid further discipline, or worse, was based on intimidation. It is not uncommon to have a suspect file a law suit to recover employment or receive financial judgements for violations of their employment or civil rights. Be cautious as to any promises or agreements that can later be considered a coercion tactic to force the suspect into cooperating.

The interviewer who has developed a reputation of being fair and impartial will be the most successful. If the interviewer uses deception and coercion to solicit confessions or cooperation, he/she will soon have a negative reputation. This may not only effect the outcome of suspect interviews, but may prevent witnesses, victims or informants from cooperating. A professional business approach to interviewing is the most effective style any interviewer can use.

GENERAL INTERVIEW CONSIDERATIONS

Interviewing has certain characteristics that are common regardless of whether the person being interviewed is a victim, witness, informant or suspect. Specific approaches to be used when interviewing in these categories are discussed separately within this section. General considerations are those that can apply to any interview situation. They may be effective in some cases and need modification in others. These considerations are offered as a guide to interviewing, with the intent of making the interview process a more successful operation.

Interview Location

The best location to conduct an interview is one that is free from distractions and provides the greatest amount of privacy. It should be comfortable and have easy access to restrooms and telephone. If possible, it should be a location that would allow access without being within view of other employees or the public. A residence, conference room or office space usually offers the ideal site.

Remember, the person being interviewed may have a reluctance to talk if other employees see him/her being interviewed. Constant distractions from noise or people coming and going in the interview location can destroy any cooperation on the part of the person being interviewed.

Confidentiality

Interviews and subsequent information obtained must be kept confidential with dissemination only to those that need to know. A person will be very reluctant, if not refuse totally, to divulge information if they feel it will become public information. This becomes almost certain if the information is embarrassing or demeaning.

If this is a concern of the person being interviewed, it is recommended that this apprehension be eliminated immediately. Telling them that information they provide will be kept confidential has to be done at the beginning of the interview process, not at the end. If the person is advised at the conclusion of the interview, information which otherwise would have been provided may have been withheld.

The same holds true with regard to records and files that are generated from the interview. Security of information is important and it should be available only to those that have a legitimate reason to access.

Conduct of the Interviewer

It is not acceptable to conduct interviews in a threatening or abusive manner. This conduct can, and probably will, result in complaints or legal suit. It is not necessary to intimidate or use abusive language in order to solicit information. Professional interviewers will not resort to questionable conduct in order to be successful. They rely on their businesslike demeanor and experience as interviewers to overcome any obstacles the situation may present. If anything, the professional interviewer has learned to have compassion and understanding regardless of whether the person is a victim or suspect.

Recording Devices

If the decision has been reached to use tape recorders during the interview, make sure this equipment is already in the interview room. The person to be interviewed may become reluctant if you begin talking, then leave the room to obtain a tape recorder. He/she may not understand your rationale for using the recorder but if already present, it's not a surprise.

He/she may still object to your recording the interview, at which time it doesn't have to be turned on. Objections to recording devices can be overcome by explaining the need for accuracy. The recording can be a true and accurate accounting of the interview, which eliminates potential mistakes when only written notes are available.

Number of Interviewers

The ideal situation is to have one interviewer. The one-on-one interview usually provides the best results. In order to develop a rapport with the person interviewed, the interviewer must be in control of the interview process. Other people present during the interview can hamper the interview by mere presence alone. Unless it is absolutely necessary, the number of people present should be restricted. It is a natural tendency for people to want to be present during an interview. This can be compounded when the person who wants to be present is the company president or your supervisor. If the need for privacy and the desire to establish rapport is properly explained to these parties, hopefully, they will comply. If this is not possible, then it may be necessary to at least restrict their questions and comments to the person being interviewed.

One main reason for restricting the number of interviewers is not to make an interview appear to be a trial. People may make statements to one they feel is not involved, but not to their supervisor or employer. This is a human response that can be expected from most people being interviewed.

Scheduling Interviews

In order to conduct an effective interview, adequate time must be made available. An estimated half hour interview could turn into a two hour interview depending upon the information provided. The person being interviewed may have a vast amount of information that takes time to detail. He/she may become emotionally stressed and a recess may be necessary. Any number of things could impact the time needed to conduct an interview. Sometimes expediency has to give way to reality.

If this is the only person to be interviewed and no additional appointments are pressing your schedule, then time has no effect. This is seldom true and the opposite is usually the case. We all have commitments and time constraints. Even if we don't, the person being interviewed may. They will seldom have the time, or care to devote the time to lengthy interviews. Tension and stress will usually wear on both parties making an effective interview almost impossible.

There is no easy solution. What may be required is an analysis of the incident being investigated for complexity or sheer volume of information needed. Combine this with the number of interviews that must be completed. These two factors may assist you in estimating the amount of time that should be devoted for the interviews. What should be avoided is having people you are going to interview wait for lengthy time periods before you can meet with them. This causes undue apprehension to develop.

If possible, allow sufficient time between interviews for relaxation and completion of notes or thoughts. All information that must be documented should be done prior to starting additional interviews. This prevents the loss of information that may have importance to the case. Relaxation between lengthy interviews is necessary, as you will find them to be emotionally draining and fatigue can become a negative factor.

Time is also an important factor when scheduling interviews. The individual to be interviewed should be given the opportunity to select a time that is convenient. Insisting on a time that matches your schedule could be met with resistance if the person to be interviewed will have to disrupt their schedule. Remember, if cooperation is being solicited, then accomodation and flexibility towards the interviewee has to be a consideration. If possible, give a time range that is broad and would easily accommodate anyone's schedule. The person to be interviewed will resist at having to lose work hours, or even worse, suffer a loss of wages. The interviewer will find out that he/she will be the one who has to have the most flexible schedule, not the person to be interviewed. It is very common for people to request a time that is either before or after work hours, enabling their interview without a need for special time-off. A note of caution should be considered when a request is made for an interview prior to normal work hours, and that is that there may not be time to complete the interview if the person being interviewed has to leave for work. The estimated time allotted for the interview may not be sufficient and valuable information may be overlooked or withheld due to time constraints. If other than normal business hours are required, then soliciting after work hours offers the best alternative. Time may not be as pressing after work as it would be prior to work. The interviewer who is considerate of the people to be interviewed will find them to be most cooperative.

Interview Attire

The professional interviewer always dresses in appropriate attire while conducting interviews. The male interviewer should have on a business suit that is not loud in color or offensive. A neutral tone is the best color to wear. The traditional shirt and tie presents the best appearance. The interviewer's clothing should always be clean and pressed. Nothing detracts from a person's appearance more than dirty and unkempt clothing. Females should wear a dress or appropriate business attire that does not call undue attention to them. Clothing that draws too much focus can cause the person interviewed to be distracted and have difficulty in keeping a clear thought process.

This topic can be difficult to discuss unless the reason for appearance is understood. The interviewer does not want the person being interviewed to be unable to concentrate on the interview. Everyone has been around or talked to individuals who wear clothing that causes attention to be directed toward them. It usually is not attractive and subjects the person to unwanted notice. If this person wants to dress in what is viewed by others as poor taste, then they must consider the consequences.

The interviewer should also keep in mind that he/she represents both the employer as well as the security professional. If a positive image is going to be displayed, it requires a certain amount of conformance to acceptable clothing standards. This may not meet with everyone's approval, but if serious thought is given to the matter, the need will become evident. A professional business image is important, as well as general expectations involving conduct and attire. If little consideration is given to attire, it could become necessary for management to address the issue with the employee. Remember, image and reputation are important factors within the business environment. Anything that causes a negative impact on the organization should be corrected. Nothing, short of job performance, has more of an impact on image than employee appearance. Projecting a positive image costs nothing. Projecting a negative image can be very costly.

CHAPTER THREE

Access Control

Access Control

A major function performed by security officers is that of access control. This assignment can range from parking control to major sporting event access. Regardless of the location or volume of activity, access control is an important function that should not be taken as routine or mundane. The importance becomes evident when it is realized that most crimes and thefts are the result of opportunity. If access to goods and merchandise is controlled, the opportunity to commit thefts is greatly reduced.

The most traditional form of access control is that of entry gate post. Companies must maintain control over access to their facilities. This is accomplished by providing physical barriers around the facility with limited points of entry or exit. It, therefore, makes access posts one of the main loss prevention techniques an organization can employ. Interior security measures are often only as effective as the controls used at access points. A lax policy of access can only result in a security system with it's effectiveness certainly compromised.

The most effective access security system can be seen as having three main components: a well documented access policy and procedure manual, a staffing policy that allows sufficient manpower and management's support and assistance in enforcing rules and regulations. With these three components in place, access control has the greatest opportunity for success.

POLICY AND PROCEDURE MANUAL

It is absolutely necessary that a policy and procedure manual be developed that spells out in a clear and concise manner, who does and who does not have access to the facility. In addition, this manual should describe in detail the procedures to follow when request for access does not meet the established policy. Prime examples would include: new employees who may not be on the authorized list, deliveries not contained on delivery schedules or emergency access requirements. This manual should be as complete as possible, yet be simple enough to follow. Complex or lengthy procedures allow for confusion and mistakes.

A policy and procedure manual should not be a well kept secret. It should be part of the overall regulations that govern the normal operating process of the organization. Every employee should be familiar with this manual and sanctions should be in place to prevent violations. The simple knowledge that access is controlled does little to ensure that adherence will be forthcoming on the part of all employees.

It is not necessary to have a voluminous section on access control. Some of the most effective policies are brief and simple enough to allow easy application to most circumstances. An example of a policy statement would be: "All visitors are required to obtain a visitor's pass prior to entry into the facility." In addition, there could be a policy that all visitor's passes are obtained from the administrative reception desk. The result is access which is easy to regulate. The policy and procedure for visitor access is contained in two single line statements.

STAFFING POLICY

Adequate staffing is the key component to any effective security program. A well designed access procedure can fail if manpower is not sufficient enough to make the system functional. If a system requires that two security officers be present, then a one-person assignment will reduce the effectiveness. The same holds true if manpower is not distributed on a basis that would allow the same level of effectiveness on any shift or time of day. It would not make sense to devote a sufficient amount of officers to a day shift, then leave other shifts without enough personnel to maintain reasonable levels of security. An example would be a facility that has four points of access/exit during business hours. Each point has a security officer who works day shift, which corresponds to peak traffic and pedestrian usage. After business hours the facility locks three entry points, leaving a single functioning gate. The closed gates are not staffed and one officer per shift is assigned to the open gate. Employees have access to the other entry points and are frequently observed using them. The fact that entry/exit would be via the open gate is known by employees, but often ignored. If, during the non-business hours, one additional officer is assigned a roving patrol duty to prevent unauthorized access at closed gates, at least a reasonable security system is operational. To rely on a single officer to provide any level of security, especially at a fixed post, is asking too much.

An access program that contains rigid staffing levels may not be economically possible. When this situation is encountered, it may be necessary to look at alternative programs that will coincide with manpower allocations. Programs that are without flexibility are going to be difficult to maintain over extended periods of time. Factors such as economics, recruitment and organizational commitment to security programs, all impact the number of personnel available or authorized. The ability to adapt and make changes in manpower deployment, will make the security program a more effective system.

MANAGEMENT SUPPORT

It is a widely accepted principle that any program not having management support has a limit to its success. Voluntary compliance is the ideal situation, but seldom adhered to by everyone. The best system is one that has the authorization and backing of supervisors and managers from all levels within the organization. If some members of the organization are allowed to violate policy and procedures, then a dual standard system is in operation. It would be difficult to enforce rules and regulations on some and not others. The result would be an impossible system to manage.

As stated previously, the security measures used do not have to be so restricting that frequent violations are a result. A simple system can be effective and allow for reasonable security functions to be employed. Management would only be required to impose sanctions against vendors or employees in extreme cases. This would be the preferable way most managers would like to handle the situation. Management support is easier to solicit when that support requires little time and effort. Remember, security is only one aspect of the total operation management has to devote time and energy towards.

Once management has approved a security access program, it is important to provide them with frequent feedback. No program is free from the need for modification as conditions change. When requesting program modifications, provide management with a brief report that outlines the requested changes, the reason for the request and authorization to implement the new procedure. This will allow management to review the report, and once approved, make the proper administrative policy modifications. This process is simple to accomplish and will go a long way in fostering an excellent relationship between the security staff and organization management.

ACCESS CONTROL CONSIDERATIONS

Techniques that can be used to control access are dictated by the physical surroundings. It can be a difficult task to incorporate officer safety into some access assignments, but this should be considered. When evaluating the control location, make sure that you take into consideration the following areas.

Physical Surroundings

The normal access control locations are such that both vehicle and pedestrian traffic use these points to enter and exit the facility. The use of fencing or other barriers funnel traffic to these locations. If this entry location is used solely for vehicle traffic and pedestrians can enter from multiple locations, then pedestrian control is out of the question. The same would hold true if the location was for pedestrians and not vehicles. Without physical barriers, access control is not an effective system, regardless of what you are attempting to control.

One of the first considerations is ensuring that the barriers are properly constructed and maintained. Locked gates that are easy to push open or crawl through have to be modified in order to avoid bypassing the intended access location. This would require an inspection of the entire facility for the purpose of locating these deficient areas. Once located and documented, it may be necessary to conduct reinspections in order to ensure that repairs or modifications have been accomplished, and are maintained in good order.

The officer's location should be such that vehicles and pedestrians cannot approach the officer at the same time. In other words, the officer should not have vehicles approaching from the front, while pedestrians are approaching from the rear. This would not be a very safe practice unless two officers are working together. A single officer cannot effectively control both vehicles and pedestrians if both are using the same access point at once. Two officers would be the ideal situation. If the security control structure is located at the access point, then it is advisable that vehicles enter on one side, usually the officer's left side where the driver's window is located, and exit on the right side for the same reason. Pedestrians should exit on the right side. This would allow for a uniform system of ingress and egress.

Lighting

It is highly recommended that adequate lighting be used before and after the fixed position. Lighting that only illuminates the officer and control structure hampers the officer's ability to see vehicles and pedestrians until they are in front of his/her location. This is also the case once they pass the entry and proceed into the complex. Remember, whatever enters will eventually exit, and thus another good reason for a lighting system that extends forward and to the rear of the entry point.

The officer does not want to be surprised by someone approaching without his/her knowledge. Adequate lighting will ease this problem by allowing better visibility.

Communication Equipment

If the location is equipped with a telephone, make sure it is operational and emergency numbers are available for your use. This equipment should not be available for public or private use, but be reserved for company and emergency business. The ideal situation is to have a combination of a telephone and radio communications, which allows a backup system in the event of a power failure.

The need for a radio communications system depends on how serviceable the other forms of available communications are. If the radio offers a better way of obtaining assistance, then this should be the first priority. It can be an unsafe practice to rely on a radio for the sole form of communications. The telephone can be the best resource if a relay process is required in order to summon police or fire assistance. The process of having a dispatcher answer your call, make telephone connection with the assisting agency, retelling the information to another operator and finally advising you of the conversation, can take a considerable amount of time. The officer could have made the call directly, instead of relying on the dispatcher and all of the extra time that entails. It is also feasible that the information given to the dispatcher could be misunderstood and, consequently, the wrong request could be relayed.

The best argument for radio use is demonstrated when it connects you with other officers. The routine transfer of information between officers, and the control of officer activity by supervisors, makes radio use the most efficient form of communications. One important factor to consider is the effectiveness of some radio systems. Quality radio systems are so expensive that their purchase and maintenance can drain the agency of valuable resources. The use of less expensive radio equipment carries with it the possibility of frequent breakdowns and poor reception. Preceding the actual purchase, it takes considerable time and research into available systems and the maintenance costs of the various systems that would meet the agency requirements, within both an economic and quality range. Radio equipment is an excellent resource for the officer to use. It should not take the place of other equipment, and by no means be regarded as the only effective form of communications. Even the best radios, unfortunately, can be ineffective in certain areas that are surrounded by buildings or natural barriers.

The previous discussion may not be construed as a positive opinion on the subject of radio equipment. This is not the case at all. Radios are important, but they do have their limitations. If the officer has ever experienced radio problems, then the concerns expressed previously would clearly be understood. The radio is only as effective as its limitations permit. To rely on one piece of equipment as the answer to all communications problems is not being realistic. Think of a radio as a tool that like any other tool can break, and frequently does just that.

Reporting Schedule

It is common to have assignments that are not only removed from other facilities, but are also difficult to reach by other officers. It is advisable to have a system in effect whereby the officer reports his/her status either by radio communications or, preferably, by personal visits from the supervisor or other officers. Telephone communication is also excellent, but in remote areas may not be available. The schedule should be one that is frequent, and at set times. This rigid schedule can serve two purposes. The first purpose is represented by an officer safety concern. If the reporting time has expired and no communications have been received, it would be an indication that a problem exists that requires immediate followup. The second purpose would indicate that the officer may not be performing the job, which would become a supervisory concern. Removed job sites can be hazardous should medical aid be required. The officer should be aware of the remoteness of the area and insist on a constant line of communications. It is one of the best methods to ensure the availability of resources and manpower should they be required.

Event Log

Paperwork is a part of our society and the need for it does not appear to be decreasing. A log of events serves to relay information to relief officers. The log includes the documenting of observations and activities that have occurred during the previous shift. The ability to remember facts and data at a later date is limited at best. It is, therefore, necessary to keep records so that situations are documented as they happen and facts are not lost to time.

A log is not an incident report. A log is usually a single-line entry that contains the date and time an event or observation occurred, along with a brief comment as to what was observed. Incident reports are much more detailed accountings of an event. They are separate from a log entry and may require a multi-paged report.

Equipment Required

All authorized equipment should be taken to the job site. Frequently, a day shift officer will forget to take a flashlight or other equipment to the job site, not expecting to use them. The officer is then required to work overtime into the night shift and, consequently, needed equipment is not available for use. The same rationale should be used with regard to clothing. It can become rather cool during evening hours, regardless of the daytime temperature and it is, therefore, better to be prepared. With regard to this issue, common sense indicates that what may not be needed at one moment could be required at the next.

It is recommended that a utility bag be acquired which would allow the storage of equipment that may be required on the job. The stored items may not be used on one job, but could be needed on another. This will eliminate the need to remember what items must be taken. The officer will always have the proper equipment at hand, not in his locker or a closet.

CHAPTER FOUR

Foot Patrol

Foot Patrol

Walking a foot beat is the most traditional form of security service. It has some positive, as well as negative aspects. Foot patrol can be one of the best customer relations tools a security organization can utilize, while at the same time it can be a costly service. Basic techniques and considerations presented can apply to most foot patrol assignments. Some forms of foot patrol cannot be accomplished without the use of radio equipment or another officer as a partner. These situations are usually officer safety issues, which are not considered as routine foot patrol. A few assumptions are made before continuing. First, assume that most foot patrol assignments are single-officer duties. Second, assume that follow-up officers are available, but usually some distance away. Third, assume that some form of communications is available for the officer to request assistance or obtain instructions.

One of the first issues that foot patrol assignments present is that of routine. One of the most difficult but important things to remember about foot patrol is not to develop a set pattern of patrolling. The first thing a pattern does is to announce to everyone where the officer will be and what time he/she will be there. If thought is given to this last statement, it will be clear why a routine style of patrol leads to an officer safety and crime prevention problem. Remember, crimes are often those of opportunity. If the officer's schedule of foot patrol is consistent and exact, it would not take long in watching to figure out the best time to commit a crime. If it is known that every hour, on the hour, the officer makes a round of the beat assignment taking forty minutes to complete, it becomes easy to plan a crime. Consider this alternative: instead of completing a round every hour, stagger the times so it appears no routine or schedule exists. For example, if a foot patrol beat takes forty minutes to complete, break it up into two twenty minute rounds. This can be done by completing the first half, then returning to the central starting point, and finally completing the second half. The next round could then be a full forty minute process. In this way, no set schedule is observed and a pattern is not obvious. This form of staggered schedule can be accomplished in many ways without difficulty. It is important to make sure that a flexible beat schedule is acceptable and authorized. If a set schedule is mandatory, then it may not be possible to implement a system of this type.

The beat officer must know if the assignment is one that requires a high visibility profile. If this form of foot patrol is desired, then it is important to maintain visibility while at the same time paying attention to officer safety. This dual consideration is at times hard to keep in balance. Officer safety should never be relaxed for the sake of job performance, yet cannot be a reason for failing to perform the assignment.

One technique to consider is advanced observation of the beat area prior to entry. If the officer takes the opportunity to observe the area from a position that is not in the open prior to foot patrolling, it could serve both officer safety and visibility requirements. This is not to say that the officer should hide in dark corners before walking into open areas. The officer can pick a point of vantage that is not within easy visibility, and just take the time to observe the area he/she is about to enter. The officer then knows who is in the area and is not subject to walking into a hazardous situation. Once this visual observation is completed the officer can complete the high profile requirements at a reduced risk.

Foot patrol requires the officer to make entry into buildings and structures, as well as open areas. Many officers forget to perform a simple safety procedure, such as turning on interior lights. It makes little sense to inspect an interior space with a flashlight, when available lighting can be used. The officer should turn the lights on as he/she enters and leave them on until departing. Remember, if someone is inside the building, they will be able to see the officer's flashlight, but the officer will not be able to see them in a darkened room. To eliminate routine, the officer may desire to leave the lights on until his/her next round. The routine of always turning the lights off when leaving is an indicator that the building is vacant. Leaving the lights on at varying times certainly raises the question of occupancy.

A classic mistake made by many officers when approaching a closed building or enclosure is to walk up to a building without taking the time to conduct a visual search. This is unsafe at best. One technique that can be utilized is the same as discussed previously on visibility. The security officer should stop prior to approaching the building and conduct a visual inspection. The officer should look for lights on inside the building, and observe whether any windows, doors or entry points show signs of forced entry or such things as screens removed. The officer should look to see if any vehicles are occupied, listen for engines running or sounds of movement within the structure. Open doors are an excellent sign that unauthorized entry has been made, and the officer must consider the possibility that the building contains suspects or unauthorized people. Entry at this time is not recommended until the police or other security officers have arrived to assist in a building search. To enter a building that shows signs of illegal entry is foolish and extremely unsafe.

Under no circumstances should the officer immediately approach a door or window when dark and look inside. From a safe distance, the security officer should shine his/her flashlight at the door or window before approaching. On approaching, the officer should not stand directly in front of the door or window. Instead, the officer should stand to either side so his/her entire body is not exposed. Consider the possibility that someone is inside and can see the officer's movements. The fewer exposed body parts, the safer the approach for the security officer.

The radio is a resource that allows quick and effective communications. Radios can also be a hazard when heard by others long before the officer arrives. Volume on radios should be sufficient for the officer to hear, but not so loud as to notify the world that the officer is approaching. Most radios have a connection for ear plugs, and it is highly recommended that these ear plugs be utilized to avoid an obvious officer safety concern.

CLOTHING REQUIREMENTS

Security officers who desire to experience the true meaning of discomfort can do so simply by wearing new shoes on a foot patrol assignment. It is unfortunate to find officers wearing shoes that were made for jumping out of aircraft, rather than for walking. It doesn't make sense that they subject their feet to this torture, but many officers insist on doing so. What they should do is purchase shoes that offer the greatest comfort, yet remain within agency guidelines for acceptable wear. You will find that comfortable shoes cost far less than "jump boots"or steel toed, seven pound tractor treads. Under no circumstances should the beat assignment be the place to break in new shoes. Common sense dictates that new shoes should be worn prior to being used on the job.

The main reason for presenting this topic is to prevent the officer from having job performance problems. It is human nature to avoid performing the job when unprepared for prevailing weather conditions. The officer who forgets a jacket, only to find it too cold to perform a foot patrol assignment, is not meeting the job requirements. This can lead to a discipline issue, not to mention the inability of the agency to provide the service they were contracted to perform.

It makes sense to assume that special clothing may be needed according to the assignment. Plan ahead. If it is used, then the right decision was made. If it was not required, nothing is lost. Be prepared for any type of assignment. There is always the possibility that a change could occur, and an inside assignment is replaced with an outside one. It may not be possible to begin a search for needed clothing, which could result in a physically uncomfortable situation.

EQUIPMENT INSPECTION

The officer who fails to properly inspect his equipment prior to use is making a serious mistake. The flashlight that does not operate during an emergency could cause injury or render the officer ineffective. The radio that has a dead battery or faulty wiring is of no value to the officer. If needed, the ability to communicate a request for assistance is not available. It is at this point that all the excuses in the world will not alter the situation. Faulty equipment can occur, however, regardless of inspection. Inspection is simply a way of reducing the chance for equipment failure. It's not a guarantee.

The routine practice of inspecting all equipment used on the job is one of the smartest things an officer can do. Allowing equipment to fail due to improper inspection or maintenance is a risk that is not recommended. The time necessary for routine inspection should not take over five minutes to complete. It's not necessary to break the equipment down into its smallest component. It can be as easy as checking the flashlight batteries and bulbs, making sure the radio battery is charged and making needed repairs to any items of clothing. This process is simple and can apply to any item of equipment the officer uses in the field.

Inspection of safety equipment requires a different approach. Never inspect weapons with other people present, or near enough to cause injury should a mishap occur. Point the weapon downward, make sure it is "on safe" and immediately unload it. It's no surprise that officers find themselves unemployed due to improper safety practices while inspecting weapons. No agency can accept the liability for an unsafe employee.

It doesn't take long to become aware of a faulty chemical mace (tear gas) container. When your eyes start to burn and tear, the cause just might be a leaky tear gas canister. Make sure that chemical mace which has exceeded its effective shelf life is destroyed and replaced with mace bearing a currently effective expiration date. The shelf life is determined by the expiration date marked on the outside of the can. Again, if that date has passed, replace it as soon as possible. The mace may still be effective, but it's not recommended that the officer take the chance.

Batons should be inspected for excessive cracks or signs of wear. It's rare that a baton will need replacement under normal use, but it doesn't hurt to inspect it along with other safety equipment. If a straight baton is used (not having a side handle like the PR-24), make sure that the rubber grommet is tight and doesn't slide easily.

The main consideration during safety equipment inspections is officer safety and the safety of others in the immediate area. Be careful, and don't rush the inspection of these items. If repairs are needed, then don't delay obtaining them. Don't use equipment that is faulty, or if you are unsure of its safety.

SPECIAL FOOT PATROL ASSIGNMENTS

The general foot patrol techniques discussed previously can be applied to the majority of assignments. However, some assignments call for individual attention to enable the officer to approach these details in a more direct manner. General foot patrol concepts can be enhanced when combined with techniques directed at specific functions.

SHOPPING COMPLEXES

Security assignments at shopping centers offer one of the best opportunities for positive relations to develop with the public. The officer must understand that maintaining positive public relations is one of the major goals of this detail. Shopping complexes are designed to provide customers with a location to purchase goods and services, not to subject the customers to excessive rules and regulations. The merchants who pay rather high rental rates need customers not only to enable them to pay the bills, but to make them a profit as well. Keep in mind anything that causes customers to go elsewhere will not be tolerated.

Security officers who work shopping centers are highly visible and, as a result, need to be very aware of their appearance. The need for a clean and spotless uniform is mandatory. The officer who has the "clean cut" look, short hair and clean shaven, usually presents the best image. This is the image desired by merchants in their security staff. When a security officer does not meet the expectations in both appearance and performance, the merchants who, directly or indirectly, pay for the service will be the first to complain.

Shopping center assignments require security officers to be service oriented, rather than focusing on the traditional security oriented aspects of the job. Security officers are expected to assist customers, more than control their conduct. It is true that control will be part of the job, but not as the main focus. Security is usually expected to use that authority only as a secondary alternative, not as a primary function. The main reason for this role is to avoid public opinion viewing shopping centers as a place where confrontations are frequent. The image the center wants to project is one of a peaceful environment, which is free from problems. After all, numerous shopping centers exist within reach of most customers. A center with a reputation as a trouble spot will find customers difficult to attract, and business will suffer as a result. Shopping center owners and the merchants who do business in these centers will accept none other than a positive customer relations policy.

Some specific functions should be considered as mandatory when assigned to a shopping center. It is necessary to make sure that the officer has a current first aid and C.P.R. certificate. It is one thing to have certification; but not to be proficient in these life saving techniques makes certification worthless. The officer must know these techniques and practice them on a regular basis. Remember, shopping centers are frequented by hundreds of people from youths to senior citizens. The possibility that illness or injury will occur to customers or employees is rather high. It is not only important to know first aid, but the security officer must not be afraid to apply these measures as the need arises. Saving someone's life is one of the greatest rewards a security officer can receive.

Security officers should take the opportunity to introduce themselves to the merchants and employees doing business in the center. This is a very positive way to develop a cooperative relationship. It is a good policy to stop and speak with these individuals and not necessarily always in a business capacity. Friendly visits can be an excellent way to build an effective relationship. One important consideration is to make sure that these nonofficial visits are brief and not disruptive to normal business operations. It is also important to make sure that such visits are acceptable policy and procedure.

The officer should know every aspect of the shopping center, including store locations, fire stations, services the center offers, business hours, special events sponsored by the center, etc. Never be caught without information that should be available for assisting and directing the shopping center customers. Complaints or other problems should be directed to the proper management official without delay or attempts to discourage the customer. It is better to resolve the issue at the proper level than to leave the customer with a sense of frustration.

The officer who confronts a negative situation should not use the public shopping center area as the place to address the problem. It is recommended that a location out of public view and hearing be utilized to resolve the complaint or problem. The center's security office or other private location should be used to discuss the issue with the person involved. Confrontations have the ability to draw attention and the situation quickly escalates. Remove the individuals to an area that is calming and not used as a public meeting room. This will usually make the customer more relaxed and easier to discuss matters with. The practice of resolving problems in public is not recommended, as it is not conducive to their effective solution. Private discussion without the additional problem of spectators makes the entire issue less dramatic.

The officer who does not like working with the public should never take an assignment in a shopping center. This officer would be absolutely miserable and would have difficulty keeping job performance at an acceptable level. There will always be customers who shop at these centers in need of information or assistance. This is common and should be considered a natural part of this job. This assignment is people oriented, and officers having the ability to effectively deal with high public contact should thoroughly enjoy this job.

One subject should be considered that has a serious impact on the public relations image shopping centers require security to project. This area concerns the philosophy of single versus two officer patrol. The public may look at two officer patrol in a shopping center as unnecessary, and feel it projects a negative image. The shopping center may attract individuals who are not shopping, but have made the center a meeting place. These individuals may cause problems, and thus, establishes the need for two officer patrol. In this case, it becomes an issue of officer safety versus image projection. This situation needs a clear policy and procedures manual that specifies the circumstances where two officer patrol is authorized. If the management prefers single patrol duties, then the officer should make sure that adequate backup is available in order to counter any officer safety problems. Remember, the center needs security, but security may have to be second to service and customer relations.

APARTMENT COMPLEX ASSIGNMENTS

Owners and managers of apartment complexes are becoming increasingly aware of the need to provide tenants and their property with security services. The compacting of large numbers of people into multi-unit apartment complexes, which are usually limited in size, creates a natural location for problems to develop. Security in these situations is designed as a property loss prevention detail. Protection of tenants, vehicles and complex property is the primary goal, with firewatch and complaint resolution being secondary.

Officers assigned to apartment complex duties need to pay special attention to developing relationships with management and tenants. Problem tenants and locations where misconduct is frequently committed are usually known by other tenants. The sharing of this information will make the security officer's job easier to accomplish. This information will not be automatically provided. It takes trust and mutual respect before any lines of communication can develop.

Public relations is the key to any effective cooperation. The officer should not feel that the service he/she is providing will automatically be met with complete acceptance, regardless of the need. The officer must maintain the opinion that he/she has to make management and tenants respect him, not the other way around. They have the right to expect a quality security service, and the officer has the obligation to provide the anticipated service. Without cooperation, it will be impossible to provide any acceptable level of service.

One important factor that should be considered is the availability of telephone communications with police and fire departments. Radio communications is an effective tool, but inside apartments or within the interior of multi-story buildings radio use may be ineffective. Try to have several telephone stations at various points throughout the complex. It would be a very unsafe practice to have communications equipment a long distance from any point the officer may patrol.

Management support of security services is absolutely necessary. The officer who attempts to enforce rules and regulations, which management has established, without management support will be totallly ineffective. Tenants and their guests would soon realize that violations would not be subject to any sanctions. There would then be no reason to comply with the officer's request. This condition creates an environment where security is in name only. It takes a dual effort on the part of security and management in order to provide any form of security protection program. Management would have to take an active involvement in security programs so that violations of rules and regulations would be addressed. The officer needs the assurance that enforcement of security procedures will be accomplished by management's immediate response. It is important that the officer advises management of problems that are worthy of reporting. Minor difficulties that do not require any form of sanctions would probably be best handled by informal counseling with the individual, or parents, if the violator is a juvenile. It is at this point that the officer's ability to develop relationships becomes important. The correction of minor problems is easy to accomplish if the officer has developed a good relationship with the tenants of the apartment complex. Good relationships means that the officer can talk with the involved parties, on a personal basis, to resolve issues. The need for formal actions on the part of management will not be necessary. This is the best way to resolve problems, especially with people the officer will be dealing with on a daily basis. The involved parties will not always comply, but the officer has taken the proper steps to resolve the issue prior to involving official complaint action.

The officer who confronts problems that are beyond his/her control, or official job duties, should immediately notify the local police for intervention and necessary action. This will prevent the officer from having to handle a situation that could result in officer injury or a continuous series of confrontations. In such situations, it is best to have the local police handle the problem. If the officer takes the time to look at the situation from an officer safety viewpoint, he/she will see that in some cases it is necesary to involve disinterested parties to resolve conflict. The police are responsible for the enforcement of laws within their jurisdiction. They do not have the requirement to remain in the same location and deal with the same people day after day. They do not have the same relationship responsibility, even though they should, as does the security officer who remains in the same area on a constant basis. It makes sense to resolve those issues that can be resolved with limited force. Those problems that cannot be addressed by other than the use of forceful means should be the responsibility of the local police agency. The officer does not benefit by engaging in activities beyond their job specifications or authority.

One major benefit of having the police involved at an early stage of any problem is the security officer's development of a positive relationship with the local police. The officer can also show the resolve of taking action to prevent any activity that is not in compliance with the rules and regulations established by the apartment management. At times, the officer may have to take such action in order to avoid future problems. Police involvement may not be the initial action desired, but once the problem accelerates to the point of a major conflict, the officer is advised to obtain the assistance of the local police department.

CONSTRUCTION SITES

Foot patrol of construction sites is a frequent security function. Builders constructing small to large projects are always subject to thefts and property damage. The cost associated with construction materials makes even the smallest project very expensive to complete. The two major types of construction consist of housing and commercial structures. Either site can be subject to vandalism and thefts from construction workers, or those who steal for resale profits. The motivation for thefts of construction items may be for use on other construction jobs, to avoid having to purchase costly materials, or selling stolen items for cash profit. The result is the same, regardless of motivation. The construction company is the victim of a theft.

The majority of construction site security jobs are during those hours construction is not in progress. Nighttime hours, weekends and holidays are normally when security is needed the most. It may appear that security is easier to provide when the site is vacant and employees are not on the job. However, the opposite can be true due to darkness, fewer people to detect criminal activity and a reduced security staff to cover large areas. This situation requires foot patrol duties to be constant, and specifically directed at antitheft measures. The officer who remains in one spot or makes only a few vehicle patrol inspections may prevent some thefts, but the likelihood is that an equal number of thefts will go undetected. The construction company finding a constant number of thefts taking place, which could have been prevented, will soon discontinue a service that is not satisfying their needs.

The officer required to patrol construction sites has to be aware of any after hours entry onto the site by employees or visitors. Any vehicle that enters should be directed to return during normal hours. If those entering the site are construction workers, the officer should have been previously informed that their entry is authorized by the construction foreman. This can be accomplished by requesting that the foreman provide you with information regarding work to be conducted after the site is closed. If possible, the information should include the area workers will be in and names of those employees authorized to be on the job site. This procedure will assist the officer in denying access to other employees not authorized to be on the job site.

Construction sites usually consist of multiple buildings and storage areas. Vehicle patrol of these areas is less effective than foot patrol, as vehicles make noise and headlights can be seen from quite a distance. Anyone intent on committing a theft needs only to wait for a vehicle patrol to pass before taking the opportunity to steal materials. Consequently, foot patrol is the best method of patrolling in these situations. The officer has the ability to make an undetected approach into buildings and storage areas. Therefore, the officer has the best chance of deterring crimes when it is observed that he/she is on foot. The criminal will not know where the officer is at any given time. This would not be the case if a vehicle is used.

The security officer must be aware that items used in construction have a very high value and, for the most part, it is difficult to prove ownership away from the job site. Ownership of stolen items, in many cases, cannot be determined due to the lack of identification markings or serial numbers stamped on the materials. Recovery of stolen property is impossible unless the officer has observed the theft, or can identify the property as belonging to the construction company. While it is not the security officer's general responsibility to take inventory or keep records, the officer should be aware of the location of records that do contain serial numbers of property so that immediate identification can be accomplished.

The officer who makes contact with the occupants of a vehicle which has entered the site should immediately make note of the license number and description of the vehicle. Make face to face contact with all occupants so that if needed at a later date, indentification of occupants can be made. Obtain indentification of all occupants and complete field interview cards on each subject. Pedestrians contacted should be identified and field interview cards should also be completed. Each of the before mentioned individuals should be requested to leave the area and be escorted in order to ensure compliance. If anything, suspicious persons or vehicles should be reported to the police to enable them to conduct follow-up investigations.

CHAPTER FIVE

Vehicle Patrol

Vehicle Patrol

Vehicle patrol provides the greatest amount of flexibility in the delivery of security services. The ability to cover large beat assignments using a single vehicle makes this form of patrol very economical. On the other hand, vehicle patrol can also be least effective in providing security based on the fact that a security officer does not physically remain at the location. The level of security required at a location will determine if vehicle patrol, though economical, will provide the best level of service.

Vehicle patrol has its share of problems and concerns. If a vehicle is not in good operating order and breaks down while in service, effectiveness comes to an abrupt halt. The purchase, maintenance, and upkeep of vehicles takes a considerable amount of resources that could otherwise be used for employment of additional personnel. The officer who drives the security vehicle may be more comfortable than the foot patrol officer, but the foot patrol officer has a single location assignment, which does not cost the agency as much in insurance premiums.

Regardless of the positives and negatives, vehicle patrol is an integral part of security and will continue to play an important role. The multipurpose functions derived from vehicle patrol make it a popular and professional method of providing competent security services. Vehicle patrol techniques are not absolutes and require the officer to adapt these techniques to the job being performed. Vehicle patrol of parking structures may require frequent stops to assist in traffic control. Patrol of large commercial buildings may require a combination of vehicle and foot patrol techniques, in order to satisfy the job specifications.

Some patrol assignments may be high visibility functions that require constant movement with little, if any, need to exit the vehicle. The main point to remember is that vehicle patrol assignments can, and frequently do, change at a moments notice. Techniques for patrolling a construction site in fair weather will not be the same as in foggy or rainy weather. The officer must have the ability to modify patrol procedures as the situations vary.

VEHICLE INSPECTION

A complete inspection of the patrol vehicle should be done prior to use. The officer should conduct a detailed inspection of the entire vehicle and equipment making note of any damage or defective components. A vehicle that has any defects that would make it unsafe to operate should not be used. In addition, a vehicle that is in violation of any vehicle code standards, even if safety is not an issue, should have corrective maintenance completed prior to use in the field. A vehicle inspection should be documented in a vehicle inspection log. This log should be simple to complete with limited time being consumed. A vehicle inspection log should have space where the officer's signature and date of inspection. A unit number and beginning mileage space should also be part of the inspection form. The officer should make special note of any defects or problems found during this inspection. Tires, body damage, lighting equipment and underbody should be inspected to ensure that the vehicle has not suffered unreported damage. Interior inspection should include brakes, steering, radio equipment and signaling devices, ensuring that they are all operational. One fact cannot be stressed enough: if the vehicle is unsafe, do not use it for field duties. Report any problems to supervision so that corrective maintenance can be performed.

OPERATORS LICENSE

Officers who do not possess a valid vehicle operators license should under no circumstances be permitted to operate a company vehicle. The officer must realize the liability he/she would be subjecting the agency to if operating a vehicle as an unlicensed driver. The agency is subject to revocation of insurance and civil damages for permitting an officer to operate a vehicle when they should have taken steps to ensure proper licensing of all employees assigned to vehicle patrol.

The officer is also at risk of being cited for operating a vehicle while unlicensed to do so. The officer's ability to continue employment without a drivers license is in serious question. If an operators license is revoked or suspended due to accidents or citations, it is in the officer's best interest to notify the agency that he/she is no longer in possession of a valid license. This is the honest approach that could save the agency and officer future problems.

SAFE VEHICLE OPERATIONS

The primary rule to follow when operating a patrol unit is safety. The officer assumes a tremendous liability both for himself and the agency when operating a vehicle during a job assignment. The potential for being involved in an accident increases with the amount of driving time the officer spends behind the wheel. The officer who practices safe driving habits while operating his/her own private vehicle will be more likely to transfer these safety habits to the job without much difficulty.

The requirement to operate a vehicle according to traffic laws does not end when driving a patrol unit. All the rules of the road apply, regardless of the reasons or rationale the officer may feel would excuse compliance. No special exceptions exist for security officers to violate any laws in the performance of their duties. To think otherwise could result in citations and fines, not to mention possible revocation or suspension of driving privileges.

The officer should look at vehicle safety from a realistic viewpoint. Involvement in vehicle code violations or traffic accidents will impact the officer's insurance and driving record. This applies whether the officer is operating a company or a private vehicle. The agency may be required to pay an increase in insurance premiums, but the same may also be true with regard to the officer's private vehicle insurance. This may seem unfair and a form of double jeopardy, but the simple fact is it can occur, over the officer's objections or personal feelings. Insurance increases do not stop when the officer is no longer employed by the security agency. These increases will probably remain with the officer for years to come.

Be smart and drive safely. It doesn't make sense for the officer to place him/herself and the agency in a position of financial liability due to unsafe vehicle operations. The officer who practices safe driving habits will be involved in fewer accidents and receive fewer traffic violation citations. Thinking safety and driving safely are two qualities that make an employee a valuable company asset.

PATROL PROCEDURES

One of the first considerations to look at is what a patrol unit represents to the general public. Many security vehicles look similar to police units. This may help in preventing criminal activity, but may also lead to a hazardous situation. Security officers may be confronted by hostile suspects who believe that a police unit has arrived, and possibly will attempt to flee by use of force. This can place the security officer in a position that wouldn't otherwise be necessary. This problem may never be adequately corrected to the satisfaction of either the security agencies or police departments. The security officer needs to be aware of this potential hazard, and use caution when approaching unknown situations.

A major mistake made by officers on vehicle patrol is to drive with the windows up and a radio on high volume. Vehicles are designed to eliminate as much outside noise as possible when all the windows are in the raised position. The officer cannot accurately hear sounds such as breaking glass or someone requesting assistance. It isn't necessary to have all the windows open, but at least have the driver's window partly open. This will allow the officer to hear sounds that originate from outside the vehicle. Some officers will not like the idea of having the window open during bad weather. It isn't safe for the officer to be unable to hear what is going on around him. This situation is one where the officer should set aside comfort for officer safety.

The opposite procedure should be used when the officer is out of the vehicle. All vehicle windows should be closed and the vehicle should be locked. This procedure will prevent anyone from damaging the vehicle interior or placing destructive objects inside. Remember, make sure the vehicle keys are removed prior to locking the doors. Place the keys in the same place at all times, usually on the officer's utility belt key ring. The officer can make a quick entry into the vehicle, without a panic search for keys, should an emergency arise.

It is impossible for an officer to make accurate observations or hear outside sounds when travelling at an excessive speed. When patrolling off-highway areas, speeds in excess of 20 miles per hour prevent the officer from being aware of the surroundings. The speed that allows the officer to do the best job is between 15 and 20 miles per hour. Remember, patrolling on public roadways requires the officer to obey the posted speed limits. There is no consent given, implied or otherwise, to impede traffic in order to perform the job assignments.

Patrol of commercial complexes can be an officer safety problem, as illustrated by the following example of incorrect prodecures: an officer enters commercial complexes with bright lights on, and immediately exits the vehicle with the radio on so loud that it can be heard blocks away. The officer walks directly up to glass windows and doors, and places his face up against the glass to look inside, then grabs the door handle and shakes the door so hard it almost breaks the glass. The officer then continues this process, going from business to business until he is so far away from his vehicle that it would take some time to reach it in an emergency.

If common sense and officer safety were considered, the officer would never use these tactics. An example of a safer technique would be the following: the officer drives by the complex before making entry to make a visual observation of any occupied vehicles, pedestrian traffic or any unusual activities. The officer could accomplish the same observation techniques by parking across the street and just observing before driving into the complex. The point is not to automatically drive into any area without advance knowledge. The officer should park close to the business being inspected, but not directly in front of it. He/she should look at the exterior for signs of forced entry or any indication that the business is occupied. The officer should then stand to the side of the windows or doors to make interior observations. Using the flashlight, the officer should look into the space with a limited amount of his/her body exposed to anyone who could be inside. Once the officer is one hundred feet from his/her vehicle, it should be moved closer to the officer's current position.

The officer should never enter a complex in the blind. It takes only a few extra minutes to make advance observations that in the long run will prevent potential hazardous situations. Think officer safety and job performance in the same context. This tactic will prove to be effective in accomplishing the goals of providing security services in a safe manner. To do anything short of this will place the officer at risk and make him/her ineffective. The agency will not be receiving the proper level of service and the potential for officer injury has greatly increased. Thinking safety is not the same as practicing safety. They must be done as one process in order to be effective.

The use of spotlights to inspect buildings or open areas presents an interesting question. Does the use of spotlights provide the same level of service as the officer exiting his vehicle and making a personal inspection? In addition, does this procedure allow the officer the same level of safety? This tactic can be debated with no real conclusion being reached. The officer who would rely on spotlights to meet the requirements of inspection would be in the wrong. The officer who never uses the spotlight to search an area would also be wrong. The best way to use the spotlight is to use it in conjunction with physical inspection. Spotlights will not always be the ideal method of doing the job. The combination of using spotlights as a tool to prevent walking into a darkened area without knowledge of anyone present, then making a physical inspection, will satisfy both needs.

Officers who are involved in vehicle patrol frequently have difficulty in keeping their equipment, mainly baton and flashlight, positioned in such a way to prevent leaving them in the vehicle each time they exit. This is a problem that can be easy to prevent. Officers should get into the habit of placing the flashlight between their legs while operating the vehicle. In this way, it is impossible to exit the vehicle without the flashlight being taken along. If the officer is right handed, the baton is worn on the left side of the duty belt. The baton should remain in the baton holder and allowed to rest between the seat and the door. If the officer would position the baton in the right manner, the baton will never be removed from the ring. The officer who is left-handed has a different problem than the right-handed officer. The baton cannot be worn inside the vehicle in a comfortable manner. It has to be removed from the holder and placed somewhere in the vehicle. There are three possible solutions: the first method is to place the baton next to the officer's right side, the second method is to place the baton between the seat and door as the right-handed officer would be doing, the third option is to place the baton between the officer's legs in the same manner as the flashlight. It is difficult to say which one of the above options is the best for the officer to consider. The best way to find the most suitable solution is to try each one. The officer can then pick the one that is the most comfortable, and which prevents the officer from leaving the baton in the vehicle. Some officers may think that the topic of where to carry a baton and flashlight is of little value. The officer who exits the vehicle without either piece of equipment may get away without needing these tools for a long time. It only takes one time for the officer to exit his vehicle without these items and find them to be required for the officer to see the importance of this topic being part of this book.

One of the greatest disadvantages to vehicle patrol is that anyone has the ability to see the vehicle and officer from a rather great distance. The use of vehicles at night almost prevents the officer from being undetected as he approaches any scene. The vehicle headlights and engine noise make it easy to observe the officer arriving. The practice of blacking out all lights prior to entering an area does not eliminate the engine noise. Remember, the advantages derived from vehicle use in patrol operations are compromised by many disadvantages that must also be considered. When the vehicle would not be the ideal method of entry to a scene or area, the officer should consider the alternative solution, which is a foot patrol entry. Don't become so attached to a vehicle that no other way is considered or utilized. The ability to be flexible and consider other alternatives to accomplish the job should not be overlooked. The officer should never allow the comfort a vehicle provides influence decisions on how a task should be performed.

GENERAL PATROL TECHNIQUES

The following general patrol techniques are offered as suggestions that should be considered during vehicle patrol assignments. These suggestions are not offered as a complete list of all options, or answers to every question. They are presented as alternative methods that should be tailored to suit the circumstances the officer encounters. The officer will find that some techniques will allow him/her to perform the job with greater competence. If these considerations and techniques can be applied with little difficulty, then they should become part of the officer's general operating procedures:

1. The officer should form the habit of constantly being aware of his/her surroundings. Don't become so involved with a single function that you forget to look around to see who is watching you.
2. Never work under circumstances where fatigue is present to the extent that it would prevent the officer from being fully aware of safety practices; thereby, compromising his/her personal safety. If the officer is too tired to perform the job in a safe manner, then the officer should not be on the job at all.
3. The officer must resist the tendency to perform the job as a routine assignment. The officer will soon begin to pay less and less attention to detail. This officer becomes ineffective and will not be capable of performing the job as expected. Routine is a problem that everyone faces, but must overcome. One solution to this problem may be assignment to other duties or job locations. This practice can be very

helpful in preventing boredom. Routine leads to boredom; and boredom leads to an unsafe officer.

4. Unless authorized, the officer should never allow anyone that is not an employee of the agency to ride-along during patrol duties. They can distract the officer and prevent him/her from performing the job properly. The officer who permits ride-alongs should be aware of the potential problems ride-alongs can pose, and take appropriate steps to prevent problems from developing.

5. The officer who has a medical limitation should not attempt to perform patrol functions that would cause him/her to become injured or disabled. If not medically suitable for the job assignment, under no circumstances should the officer attempt to perform the job. It is better to request a job assignment that the officer is capable of handling.

6. Don't be embarrassed to ask questions when you do not understand something. To get clarification is the best way to resolve the problem. This policy of asking questions for problem resolution can prevent the officer from providing a patrol program that does not meet the job specifications. The main criteria is that the officer knows the job requirements and can direct his/her energy towards fulfilling these requirements.

7. Practice a policy of community relations in all contacts with citizens and customers. The officer who has developed a good relationship with people is one who is not only effective, but pleasant to work with. It does not take any special effort to be friendly or polite, however, it does take energy to be contrary.

8. Under no circumstances should the security officer attempt to be something he/she is not. To function as a police officer when this isn't the case is not only a violation of the law, but a serious officer safety concern as well. This is not an issue to debate. The bottom line is unless the officer has police powers and authority, using them can cause the officer to be subject to legal and civil penalty.

9. Should the officer confront a situation that amounts to a violation of the law, the officer should not attempt to resolve

the issue. The local police is the authority that has jurisdiction over law violations and they should immediately be contacted and assisted when possible.

10. Use every opportunity to gain knowledge and experience on how to perform the job in a more competent manner. To resist change or refuse to accept a better way of handling a situation is not in the best interest of the officer or the profession. No one has all of the answers to all of the questions. Take the opportunity to learn by watching and listening to other officers who have more experience, and are willing to relate information.

11. The security officer should never develop a habit of patrolling his/her beat in the same pattern. It is important to vary the patrol pattern in such a way that the officer accomplishes the job, but does not allow anyone to know the exact time to expect the patrol. The need to use alternative times and direction of travel is important. The officer who arrives at a location the same time each night and takes the same route to that location is establishing a pattern that could present an officer safety problem. The officer may consider arriving at the location and completing the security inspection as normal, then immediately after leaving the area make a surprise return, and conduct an additional inspection. Any variation of this process can accomplish the same goal. The officer may arrive early or remain longer at the location, which would be a different approach. Remember, vary the patrol schedule so that a pattern does not appear to exist.

12. The officer should become familiar with the beat assignment and location of such as: hospitals, police departments, fire and rescue, gas stations that are open and any other public or private service organization. This beat familiarization technique will allow for assistance to be obtained, and provide the officer with the ability to refer citizens to services should they be required. This knowledge will serve as an excellent community relations tool, and an emergency resource for the officer.

13. The patrol officer should report any problems that are found on the beat to the immediate supervisor, so that any corrective action can be taken. Problems do not have to relate to the officer's own job; but may relate to a business such as: a broken window, bushes being too high around a residence which prohibits an unobstructed view of windows or doors, a business leaving mail lying on the floor which signals that no one has been in that day, lights that have burned out in parking lots or delivery bays, or any other observation the officer makes that would serve to make the job easier to accomplish or would help the business prevent thefts or vandalism.

14. The beat officer should make every effort to meet business owners and employees who are present during the officer's patrol time. These employees and owners are the best resource for information and assistance should it be needed. The community relations effect of being seen and showing interest in their safety cannot be overlooked. The officer who takes the time to be looked upon as a service provider, and not just security, will realize the benefits of this time being well spent.

15. The officer who has a high crime patrol area may have to consider the use of a two-man unit. This additional officer may prevent a hazardous situation from becoming a reality. However, the two-man unit does entail additonal cost and use of a two-man unit does not become an enforcement unit. Enforcement is not the intent of the security patrol system, prevention of criminal activity and protection of property is the purpose of patrol functions. The addition of another officer is for the safety of the beat officer, and not indicative of altering the goals and objectives security is intended to achieve.

16. One of the most effective ways to develop a good working relationship with the local police is to make a personal visit to the police department. The security officer should introduce him/herself to the watch commander who is working the same work schedule the officer is assigned. The officer should let the watch commander know how he/

she can be reached, and the area the officer is assigned. This will allow the development of a mutual understanding, and respect for each other's role and responsibilities. The watch commander will relay this information to the officers who are in the field, so that the security officer's presence will be known. It is also advised that the officer make an attempt to talk to the police officers who are working the same beat. This will also help develop a good working relationship. Remember, these are the officers who provide follow-up assistance if the officer encounters a hazardous situation. A positive result of this communication is the exchange of information that can occur when the officers officially and unofficially meet. This information exchange can prove valuable to both parties.

17. The vehicle patrol officer must remember that his/her public visibility far exceeds that of the foot patrol officer. This fact focuses attention on some areas the officer must consider. The officer may pay special attention to driving habits that would be viewed as negative or cause attention to be directed toward the officer. The unit being driven by the officer will probably have identification that advertises the agency he/she works for. Any negative driving habits will be a direct reflection on the company, as well as the officer. The agency certainly does not want negative opinions of their organization to be brought about by one officer's poor driving habits. The officer who tailgates, drives too fast, cuts other drivers off, makes offensive gestures towards other motorists or expects special consideration will soon find out that this conduct is unacceptable, and will probably result in complaints to the employing agency. To avoid this, the officer must pay special attention to driving habits that would foster a positive image of the officer and agency.

18. The security officer on vehicle patrol must be aware that they represent a form of authority that will not be accepted by all those they come into contact with. The officer must also understand that this is something that will occur and must be addressed. The recommended solution to the problem isn't easy to remember, especially when the officer

has done nothing to warrant any negative feelings. The natural tendency is to respond in a negative way that would counter the abuse being received. This is not the best way to handle the situation. The best way to respond is not to respond at all. Negative reception to the officer is expected and has to be considered as an issue that may arise. Take the situation as being a response to your authority, not to you as a person. It's rare for a negative encounter to be directed at the individual personally. It usually relates to the officer's positon, not to the person who holds the position. Keep this concept in mind. It will help in avoiding a no-win situation.

19. Appearance is almost as important as the job the officer is performing. The officer who is neat and clean in appearance, who has clean equipment, including his vehicle, will project the desired image of a professional security officer. The officer must realize that appearance will have an effect on preventing confrontations and increasing his/her overall effectiveness. The officer will find that his/her appearance has a dramatic impact on ability to perform the assigned task. The most effective officer will be the one who takes pride in appearance, and works towards keeping these standards at all times.

20. The officer who keeps the customer's interest in mind will find that in general the job is easier to accomplish. The officer should bear in mind that protection of the customer and his property is the single most important aspect of the assignment he/she can fulfill. A business owner expects the officer to take a personal interest in providing the service he/she is paid for. The officer who concentrates his/her time and energy toward fulfilling these expectations will find that problems will, as a result, be more easily resolved. This is a consequence of the interest and dedication the security officer has invested in his/her assignment and his/her efforts toward providing an effective service.

CHAPTER SIX

*Crime Scene
Containment*

Crime Scene
Containment

The security officer has an obligation to contain a crime scene in order to prevent contamination and destruction of evidence. Once a crime scene is discovered, certain steps must be taken that will allow the scene to remain undisturbed. The containment process will be determined by the type of scene, the size of the scene, the current or immediate weather conditions and the possibility of contamination by individuals or equipment. It isn't necessary for the officer to be a specialist in crime scene investigations. If proper techniques are used, a crime scene can be contained until the criminalist has the opportunity to conduct a scientific investigation. It is important to remember that crime scene investigations is a science, and not a casual occupation. It takes years of specialized training before anyone can be qualified as a criminalist. The goal of the security officer is containment, not examination of the crime scene. The following crime scene suggestions represent the most frequent crime scenes that the officer will be required to contain. The officer should remember that many major crimes are solved by evidence collected at crime scenes, not by eyewitnesses or confessions from suspects. This should serve to reinforce the need for adequate crime scene containment.

POLICE NOTIFICATION

The location of a crime is the crime scene. The scene may consist of multiple sites and extend for a considerable distance. The criminal who commits a theft at one location and drops items on the escape route would create multiple scenes. The area surrounding each dropped item would constitute a separate crime scene. The officer may be aware of the first crime scene, but not the others. It is for this and other reasons that the police must be immediately notified of a crime so an extended search, at and beyond the scene, can be conducted. One reason to have police respond, as soon as possible, is the potential need for a crime scene specialist. These specialists are only available at police request and, seldom, if ever, at the request of private agencies. Bomb disposal teams, hazardous chemical squads and arson investigators are examples of the types of specialists that may be required.

Police arrival may start a chain of events that can result in swift apprehension of the suspect. Remember, the criminal will rarely remain at the scene of the crime. They usually attempt to flee in order to avoid detection and arrest. This situation normally puts the suspect well beyond the boundaries of the security officer's area of responsibility. The jurisdiction of the security officer does not permit the extension of the investigation beyond that permitted by agency policy and criminal law.

BOUNDARY CONTAINMENT

The first step in containment is to put a physical barrier around the crime scene. This barrier can be plastic tape on which a warning, prohibiting entry of the area, is written. The use of additional security officers, positioned around the scene to prevent contamination, is also an effective technique. The use of officers is more expensive, but does offer more security than the use of tape or other barriers which can be easily circumvented.

A structure or enclosure can be secured by closing the doors, and putting the plastic tape across the entry points. Windows that are not locked should also be taped to prevent entry or contamination. A crime scene that involves a street or intersection may require a complete closure to prevent unauthorized entry by pedestrians or vehicles. Large open areas are the most difficult to control. It may be necessary to request additional officers to assist in containment.

Vehicles can be sealed with tape, or an officer can be posted at the scene to prevent access or movement. Vehicles, and for that matter most scenes, are easily contaminated by the officer when he/she does not take care in handling evidence, and inevitably disturbs it. Unless absolutely necessary, never enter the interior of a vehicle to secure it. Exterior sealing is the best method of securing a vehicle. Tape can be wrapped around a vehicle without having to touch any surfaces that may contain fingerprints or other evidence.

Small items of evidence that may be located outside the main crime scene can be covered with a trash can or other cover that does not actually touch the item. An example of this situation would be: A store window has been smashed and the suspect takes the display items. While running to a waiting vehicle, the suspect drops a bracelet that may contain fingerprints. The store front is sealed to prevent any contamination and a single officer can control access. The bracelet is important evidence, but is located forty feet from the main crime scene. To avoid the evidence being destroyed or tampered with, the officer can place a hollow object, such as a trash can lid or empty box, over the bracelet. The officer can then maintain visual security over the object without having to leave the main crime scene. This is a simple example, but represents how easily some items, that are distant from the primary crime scene, can be controlled. This technique may work in some situations, but not be very practical in others. It will take the officer's assessment of the situation to determine what measure will be the most practical to use under the circumstances.

Blood stains or other liquids require special handling. The best thing to do is provide a barrier around the liquids without having to touch them or cause contamination. Many liquids are toxic chemicals that can cause harm to those that come into contact with the substances. Don't take any chances with the unknown liquids. Contain them, then obtain assistance from the experts that specialize in hazardous or toxic substance. Large liquid spills are difficult to contain. It may be impractical to place tape or other objects around the area. In this case, additional manpower offers the best solution. These officers can be positioned around the scene to prevent contamination or exposure.

CRIME SCENE DIAGRAM

The officer should make a diagram of the scene, with special attention paid to the location of evidence. This diagram should be accurate and have the capacity of being easily understood by anyone reading it. The diagram should be signed and dated by the officer, in the event it becomes evidence for later court action. The diagram does not have to be an artist's rendition of the scene. It can be a simple drawing that represents the officer's observations and findings as he/she surveyed the scene.

When the police arrive at the scene, the security officer should make sure the diagram is provided to them. The diagram may be of value to their investigation and could prove to be supporting evidence. The best evidence rule states that the original document should be the document that is offered as evidence. If the security officer needs a copy of this diagram, xerox it or make a duplicate. Make sure the authorities receive the original so it cannot become lost as time passes.

CRIME SCENE PHOTOGRAPHY

When possible, the officer should photograph the crime scene as it is discovered. This requires the officer to carry a camera that takes instant photographs, not one that requires development at another location. This will permit the officer to attach photographs to the crime scene diagram. These two items combined will show the crime scene as it was when the officer arrived. Photographs are excellent items of evidence. Photographs can dispute testimony by suspects, and help in providing a clear picture of what occurred.

The officer who takes the time to photograph crime scenes will find out how easy it is for individuals or equipment to destroy these scenes. Simply walking around the scene can destroy evidence and disrupt the original condition. Photographing the scene is one way of keeping it in its original state, even if some items of evidence have been moved or altered. The photograph can allow the scene to be reviewed for possible tampering or altering. The officer should take the time to photograph scenes as one of the first priorities.

ACCESS TO CRIME SCENES

Once the crime scene is contained, it is important to restrict access to any unauthorized persons. Access should be denied to anyone without proper authority, regardless of their position or status. Denial to some people is difficult to accomplish. Business owners and agency supervisors may request or demand to enter the crime scene. At this point, a real problem can develop. The best way to handle this situation is to request their cooperation in remaining outside the scene until the police have arrived and given permission for them to enter. If this is not acceptable and access is insisted upon, then access may have to be granted. Document the access with the persons name and their stated reason why access was necessary. It maybe difficult for some officers to understand why access must be granted to certain people. First of all, you do not have the authority to deny a business owner access and his/her own property. Supervisors may exert their authority and order you to allow them access. In these cases, common sense will have to take over. Allowing them access will immediately release you of the responsibility of the scene containment. This fact should be explained to them, in order for them to realize that their actions will result in their assuming responsibility. If this is not effective, then you have done your best to contain the scene.

The general public has no right to enter a crime scene. The officer will be approached with any number of reasons why they should be allowed to enter the scene. They may insist that the owner would not mind, or that they are friends of the victim. None of these excuses, as presented, should be taken as authorization to allow them access to the scene. It will, at times, be difficult to overcome the emotional state that some victims or friends will display. It isn't necessary to react to these emotions, in fact, a neutral and unbiased reaction would be the appropriate response. The officer should be understanding and sympathetic, but should not show any bias or express any opinions or conclusions on his/her part. Later evidence may prove to be such, that what appeared to happen is not what actually occurred. Involvement in these situations should be limited to job related functions. Taking sides or offering suggestions can lead to involvement, far beyond providing a service, and you can actually become a party to the incident. This is not the role the officer was hired to perform.

Once the proper authorities have arrived on the scene, and all of the information and details have been provided to them, then the security officer has released containment into their custody. Quite frequently the officer is requested to remain at the scene and assist the police in controlling the area. If approval from the supervisor is obtained for the security officer to remain, then it is recommended that this be done. The positive relationships that can develop from assisting the police officer far outweighs the expense of having the officer remain for a few hours. The officers working the crime scene are usually the beat officers who patrol that area. It cannot be stressed enough just how important it is to have a working relationship with the officers who will be responding to assist the security officer in time of need. It will pay off in the long run, while at the same time letting the local police know that the officers at that location are willing to assist them in a professional and competent manner. This mutual trust can be a very positive method of developing a relationship that will mean a sharing of information and respect for one another's role.

It is so important for the security officer, and the police for that matter, to understand that no one can work in a vacuum. At one time the police may need the security officer's assistance; and the next time, the security officer may need the police officer's assistance. The development of a good working relationship will permit both parties to work together in a manner that allows both to perform their jobs more effectively. If this subject is given the proper consideration, it will be easily understood just how important a little cooperation from both sides is, since it will result in the best possible working environment.

CHAPTER SEVEN

Report Writing

Report Writing

The ability to accurately document a crime or incident is so important that report writing is presented in its own section. The officer must have a thorough understanding of the report writing process so that each report will contain information that represents a clear and concise description of what occurred. When a report is completed, it begins a chain of events that may include future review by police, attorneys and judges. It is common to find a report written years ago currently being used in a trial or judicial hearing. The information contained in a report becomes a permanent record that will be subject to recall and use long after the officer has forgotten the incident. A report can reflect a positive or negative opinion depending upon the reporting officer's attention to detail and the process he/she used to arrive at conclusions. When the officer writes a report that is unclear or vague, the reviewing official does not have the opportunity to make a value decision. The report does not accomplish the goal of providing a document that explains what occurred, when it occurred, how it occurred, why it occurred or who was involved. These elements are necessary in order to have a complete report.

The best way to approach report writing is to start with field note taking. Field note taking is separate from report writing, in that the field notes are usually the foundation for the actual report. Field notes are used to develop the final report with supporting information added for clarity. The officer who develops effective note taking techniques will find that writing reports becomes easier and less time consuming.

FIELD NOTE TAKING

Field note taking should not be confused with transcription of taped interviews or other predocumented information. Field notes are derived from interviews and observations the officer makes while conducting field assignments. The most common form of field notes are taken from victim interviews, crime scene observations, witness interviews and telephone conversations with individuals who have information about an incident or crime. It is also important to look at field notes as being the officer's foundation for followup interviews and investigations. The officer discovering information that would lead him/her to other persons having knowledge of the crime will have the field notes to use as a basis to ask the right questions or conduct interviews. The original notes may not contain sufficient information to complete a report, but combined with other interview notes, a complete report could be made. The following is an example of this concept: A witness has advised the officer that he discovered his neighbor's house has been broken into. The officer has the witness' statement, but not the victim's statement indicating an actual crime has been committed and the amount of loss suffered. The officer uses the witness' statements as the reason for contacting the victim. The victim's information combined with the witness statements provide sufficient data that would allow a complete report to be written. The witness' statement alone was not sufficient to complete a report. The combination of the two made it possible to answer all the necessary questions that could arise.

Notes taken as a result of information obtained during field contacts need not be so lengthy that a report is almost written. The officer can make single line entry, or a reduced accounting of the incident. These notes should be such that the officer can look at them at a future date and be able to accurately recall the event. What has happened to everyone at sometime or another is finding a note entry that doesn't prompt recollection. In fact, the officer finds it impossible to remember the reason for writing the notes in the first place. This makes note taking little more than an immediate tool with limited future value. The ability to prompt a recall of the interview or observation is the key element in note-taking. The officer who writes adequate information that allows him/her to read the notes and be able to remember statements made, or observations of the scene, has accomplished the goal of note-taking. Sufficient, yet limited documentation that permits future recollection, of both a short to a long time span, will make note-taking one of the most valuable abilities the officer can possess.

The officer should strive to develop a note-taking system that is comfortable and easy to remember. One technique is to take information and break that data into main and subtopics. This permits the officer to take a main subject, and add information that relates to that main topic directly underneath. The following example is provided as a means of clarification:

I. First main division of the subject
  A. First significant point relating to or supporting "I".
    1. Important item related to "A"
      a. Data related to "1".
      b. Additional data related to "1".
        (1) Further explanation of "b".
          (a) Detail related to "1".
II. Second main division of the subject.
  A. First important point relating to "II".
    1. Further explanation of "A".
  B. Second significant point pertaining to "II".
    1. Additional explanation of "B".
    2. More about "B".
  C. Third significant point pertaining to "II".
III. Third main division of the subject.
  A. First important point relating to "III".
    1. Further explanation of "A".
      a. Data related to "1".
        (1) Further explanation of "a".

The above system is standard college note-taking format. The officer who utilizes this format will find that with use, it becomes a simple, yet effective way, to document an incident or interview in an abbreviated manner. This process permits notes to become the basis for the final report. The following information is provided to show how this system can work, and how it can be utilized to assist the officer in developing effective note-taking techniques:

I. Residential burglary.
   A. 2345 Main Street
      1. Victim: Robert and Edith Jones.
         a. M.O. window smash.
         b. Rear window.
            (1) Bedroom window.
      2. Time burglary occurred: 2340 Hours
      3. Broken window only physical evidence found at scene.
II. Reported loss valued at $3,000.
   A. Television set.
   B. Stereo components.
   C. Jewelry.
      1. No serial numbers available.
      2. Jewelery not significant.
III. Witnesses.
   A. Earl Robertson.
      1. 2343 Main Street
      2. Lives S/O victim
   B. 2340 Hours heard noises from alley behind victim's residence.
      1. Saw M/W/A Bln Hair Dark clothing exit rear yard.
      2. Heard vehicle leaving.
         a. Vehicle had bad muffler

The officer who wrote down these limited notes can then recall the supplemental information obtained from the victim or witness to include in the final report. The following report represents how this information is correlated into the completed documents:

On 5-1-88 at approximately 0025 hours I responded to 2345 Main Street to investigate a reported burglary. On arrival, I contacted victim Robert Jones who is the victim/owner of the residence. Jones advised me that on

4-30-88 he returned to his residence to find his neighbor, Mr. Robertson, shining a flashlight at the front of his residence. Jones said that he was advised by Robertson that he heard the sound of breaking glass coming from the rear of his residence. Jones said that Robertson exited his residence to observe a male white adult with blonde hair and wearing dark clothing run from the rear of his residence and jump the rear fence. Jones then said that Robertson heard a vehicle exit the rear alley at a high rate of speed and sounded like the vehicle had a broken muffler. Jones said that he immediately entered his residence to find it had been burglarized. Jones said that Robertson is at his residence and would be available for interview.

Jones then escorted me into the residence where I was shown the master bedroom which is located in the extreme northeast corner. I observed the bedroom to be ransacked with drawers and personal belongings lying all over the room. I observed the N/E corner window to be broken with glass lying directly underneath. Jones then directed me to a wooden stand where he said a television was located when they left for the evening. Jones also showed me the location where the stereo unit was located which is approximately four feet (4) south of the broken window. Jones then directed me to a jewelry box located on top of a dresser which is located directly underneath the broken window. The box was opened and contained inexpensive jewelery, with additional jewelery lying around the open box. Jones then advised me that a check of other rooms in the house showed no signs of tampering. Mr. Jones was not able to provide any information or description of the stolen items, but said his wife would be able to offer better details.

I then contacted Mrs. Edith Jones who stated that on 4-30-88 she and her husband were visiting relatives from 1600 hours to approximately 2400 hours. Mrs. Jones said that around 2400 hours they returned to find Robertson in front of their house with a flashlight. Mrs.

Jones said she did not talk with Robertson but did hear him say he heard glass breaking from the rear of her residence. She said she entered the house and found the broken window and the television set, stereo unit and jewelery missing. Mrs. Jones said she did not have serial numbers or brand names for the television set or stereo. She said the jewelery was not special made or have any unique design. Mrs. Jones was able to provide me with an estimated loss for the items stolen:

1. Television set $ 900.00
2. Stereo unit   600.00
3. Jewelry   1500.00
                        _____
            Total: $3000.00

I then completed my interview with the victims at which time I made a search of the rear yard of the residence to find no physical evidence present. I then interviewed Mr. Robertson who stated that the information Mr. Jones provided was accurate. Mr. Robertson said he was sure the time he heard the noise of the glass breaking was 2340 hours due to the fact that he had just looked at his watch. Robertson then stated he would not be able to identify the suspect if seen again because he had only seen the suspect from the rear and did not see his face.

Based on interviews and observations this officer concludes that on 4-30-88 at approximately 2340 hours an unknown suspect broke into the Jones residence and removed the listed property. The suspect is unknown with no independent witness able to identify him. The point-of-entry was a bedroom window and only one room appears to have been burglarized. Pending additional information and/or witnesses to the crime, the case is without leads or any follow-up recommendations.

The previous report represents a finalization of interviews and observations the officer made at the scene of a burglary. The report was developed from the limited information the officer found at the scene, and documented in his/her field notebook. It was not necessary for the officer to write the report while conducting interviews or making observations. The field notes allowed the report to be written at a later time.

The previous example could have been expanded to include additional information the officer may have documented in his field notes. The ability to reduce or expand information needed to complete a report is built into this note-taking system. The officer could have several lines of information under a subtopic or single statement. If the officer can recall details with limited entry of information, then short statements will be adequate. If more detailed information is necessary to prompt recall, then the officer will need to lengthen the amount of data contained in his/her field notes. Remember, this is a format, not the solution to a problem. The officer must determine what information will be required. Officers who have a difficult time remembering details may have to write more than the officer who can remember information with limited entries. The system should be adapted to the officer's own personal abilities and limitations.

Field notes should never be destroyed. Once used, they should remain in the officer's notebook, or be stored for future use. If the officer decides to keep the notes as part of a daily notebook, then he/she should make sure each entry is dated. Once the notebook is full of information, it should be stored in a location that will be available for ready reference or review.

Notebooks range in size from small, pocket size to legal size tablets. It's the officer's own preference that should dictate the size that would best suit the circumstances. A small pocket size offers the best notebook when limited information is required. Large sizes may offer the best solution if longer or more complex notes are needed. One way the officer can accomplish a balance is by carrying a small notebook, while a large one is contained in his/her briefcase or equipment bag. The small notebook would be sufficient for normal interviews or observation entries. The larger notebook would then be available for use in major cases or crime scenes.

REPORT CONTENTS

It's no secret that report writing is the most difficult function officers must perform. Over one hundred books exist that try to explain how to write a report. Some books try to teach an English course, while others attempt to direct the officer through a maze of information which is not understood or is too difficult to put into practical use. After all, a report is a document that relays information and tells a story. It is not writing a textbook or mystery novel. A report should be a document that contains a clear, and concise representation of a crime or incident. This report should permit the reader to understand what occurred, with little or no need to ask questions. Reports become difficult to write when the officer writing the report forgets to obtain necessary information that makes it a complete document. Writing a report that is incomplete may be of limited value to anyone who reads it, or must use it for follow-up investigation. Questions will be unanswered, and someone else may be required to complete the entire process, in order to make the report a usable document.

The officer who writes the report must consider what he/she is trying to accomplish. A report must contain those elements that show a crime or event did occur. It should contain statements or observations that have a direct relationship to the crime or incident. Statements should be based on direct interviews by the officer, not relayed from a third party. Observations should represent the officer's observations, and not what another person perceives. Officer obtained information eliminates the possibility of someone else providing false, or misleading statements that are presented as an accurate accounting of another's testimony. It's possible that this data represents a version that has been elaborated upon, or has eliminated vital information pertaining to the actual comments. If the officer documents only information that he/she has obtained, the report should not be subject to criticism.

A complete report will have to contain the Who, What, When, Where, Why and How elements. A simple example would be a report that contains an officer's observations of a crime and subsequent arrest:

On 5-1-88 at 2300 hours while on foot patrol of McCullars construction site, I observed a 1985 Ford pickup truck, license number 123ABC enter the construction storage area without the vehicle headlights on. I observed the vehicle to contain a single occupant, later identified as James, Robert Allen, 167 Main Street, Los Angeles, Calif., 90006, with a date of birth of 3-6-44.

I approached the vehicle and from approximately fifty (50) feet away, observed James exit the vehicle and look from side-to-side. James then walked to the N/E corner of the storage area and picked up two (2) circuit boards that were stored on an open wood pallet. James then walked back to his vehicle and placed the circuit boards in the rear of the truck's open bed.

I contacted dispatch and requested the police be notified that a possible theft was in progress. The vehicle and suspect description was given and the exact location within the construction site was provided. Dispatch advised me that the police were enroute with an estimated time of arrival of approximately five (5) minutes.

I observed James walk back to the stacked circuit boards and remove two (2) additional boards and place them inside the cab area. James was observed to be looking around at all times which appeared to be an attempt to detect whether anyone was approaching or observing him. James then entered his vehicle and began backing out of the site. It was at this point that the police arrived and stopped James as he backed onto First Street.

Police officers Roberts and Black contacted the suspect and had him exit the truck. Officer Roberts contacted me and my observations were provided. I observed the officers removing the circuit boards from the suspect's vehicle then place him under arrest. Officer Roberts advised me that James admitted the theft and was going to resell the items for cash. The serial numbers of the circuit boards were obtained and Officer Roberts took custody of the boards as evidence along with James' truck.

Mr. Alan McCullars arrived at the construction site and provided the police with the necessary information as the victim of the theft. Mr. McCullars advised the police that prosecution of James was desired. This case was closed by arrest and recovery of the stolen property.

In reviewing this report, the officer was able to incorporate the Who, What, When, Where, Why and How elements:

1. Who: Suspect James, Robert Allen
2. What: Committed a theft of circuit boards
3. When: On 5-1-88 at 2300 hours
4. Where: McCullars construction site storage area
5. How: Removes circuit boards and places them in this truck.
6. Why: Personal gain.

These elements, when included, make a report complete as to necessary primary information. By providing these elements, any report will be complete and to the point. It is important to ensure that any report includes these elements. When any element is missing, it results in an incomplete report and will not satisfy the need for an accurate accounting of a crime or event. Consider these elements when any report is written. They represent the basis of a report that answers any possible questions pertaining to what occurred.

REPORT WRITING STYLE

The use of repetitive designation, such as: "This Officer", "The Undersigned", or "Officer Jones", soon becomes awkward and difficult to read over and over in a report. It isn't necessary and makes a report boring to read. It's not a crime to write a report in the first person. "I" is acceptable and eliminates lengthy and repetitive wording. "I observed the suspect remove the property" is a direct statement that leaves little doubt as to who made the observation. The use of "I" makes more sense than using "The Undersigned Officer", every time the officer begins a statement or sentence. To constantly read, "The Undersigned Officer" will soon make reading the report such a chore that attempting to gain knowledge of facts surrounding a case becomes of secondary importance.

If writing reports using "I", representing the reporting officer, is acceptable with supervision, then it is recommended. "I" is simple to use and relieves some unnecessary wording. The officer will find that reports will be easier to write, and it will be less difficult to present information in a clear fashion. To write a report that requires re-reading several times to achieve clarity is not a report, but a test of patience. Make reports simple and easy to read. You will appreciate this as much as those who will review and process your reports.

CHAPTER EIGHT

Use of Force and Weaponry

Use of Force
and Weaponry

The decision regarding when to use force and when it's not appropriate to use force is one of the most debated subjects in the law enforcement and security field. The issue becomes even more complex when a decision to use force is subject to judicial review long after the event occurred. The alleged victim of force can file suit against the officer and agency, and even the manufacturer of the weapon or instrument used. In addition, be aware of the fact that law suits may not even address the weapon or instrument used, but only infer that the amount of force used was excessive under the circumstances. In order to complicate the issue even further, a law suit dealing with force issues can also be against the supervisor of the officer who used the force, the agency who hires the officer, and the school that instructed the officer in the use of the weapon.

It's no wonder that a policy and procedure for the use of force is very broad and full of recommendations rather than direct instruction. It's impossible to take every variable that could exist into consideration when developing a use of force regulation. Take for example a policy that states: "The officer shall only draw and use a firearm in extreme emergency situations that could result in death or serious injury to the officer or private citizens." This policy statement appears to be rather direct. The officer can use a firearm in extreme emergencies. Now look at the issues involved in this policy. Who really determines when an extreme emergency exists? What constitutes an extreme emergency, versus just an emergency? How does the officer know a situation could result in death or serious injury? You could reason that the officer's experience and training will determine the answer. Does that mean a new, less experienced officer will never have to make such decisions? What if the suspect is not armed but behind the wheel of a vehicle, and says that he will run over innocent victims if he is not allowed to leave? Does an extreme emergency exist at this point, or after he runs over several people? These questions demonstrate the difficulty and confusion in use of force issues. A hundred more examples could be provided, but the results would be the same. The officer must take use of force guide lines into consideration when he/she is faced with a use of force situation. The individual officer must make the decisions on the use of force, while at the same time taking into consideration policy and the immediate circumstances involved in the particular incident.

The previous discussion concerned the use of a firearm. Most people consider it the ultimate limit of force. The use of nonlethal force such as the baton, chemical mace and physical restraints can also result in the same actions being brought against the officer. As an example, the officer who uses a baton during an altercation that results in a severe injury to the victim's head, ultimately causing death, is in the same situation as the officer who used a firearm. The issue would relate to whether the force used was warranted or not under the circumstances. In addition, the officer who has no physical contact with the suspect but uses nonlethal chemical mace can also be subject to law suit. To illustrate this point; the suspect falls to the ground while reacting to the effects of mace, and suffers injury due to the fall. Again, the issue would relate to whether or not the use of mace was warranted under the circumstance.

At this point, it should be quite evident that the use of force can be of no win situation, no matter how restrained the officer was in using it. The officer who uses common sense, and responds with only that force necessary to overcome resistance, can still be subject to judicial review of his/her actions many years from the time of the original incident. It is one thing to be held accountable for a decision by supervision that was present at the scene during the incident, or shortly after. It is something else entirely to be judged years later, and by someone who was not present or never had to experience similar situations. The suspect's combative condition, the availability of witnesses to testify, and the officer's attempts to resolve the issue in a peaceful manner all seem to be lost as time and emotional involvement has passed.

The officer who accepts employment in the security profession must also accept the fact that the potential for using some level of force is part of the job. The officer may never use force that even comes close to being considered lethal. The officer may only be required to use simple commands, or restraining holds to satisfy the job requirements. Whatever level of force is required, the officer has to respond within guidelines based on policy and reasonableness. To act outside the boundaries of either factor puts the officer in a position where punitive action is almost certain.

The officer has to follow agency policy and procedures which govern the use of force. These regulations must be clearly understood to enable the officer to act according. If any policy or procedure is not clear, the officer must obtain clarification immediately. The officer who knows the limits and situations where force is authorized can then incorporate the reasonableness standard into the picture. Reasonable force is that force necessary to overcome resistance. Reasonable force may also be that force necessary to prevent bodily harm to the officer or private citizen. Reasonable can best be defined as that action which the majority of people would have taken under similar circumstances.

Excessive force is that force used which exceeded the amount necessary to permit the officer to overcome resistance or prevent injury. The officer who uses deadly force, in a situation not warranting such force, is using excessive force. The officer who uses a baton to overcome resistance, but continues to use force once resistance has been overcome, is using excessive force. Example after example could be used to explain the concept of excessive force. But these examples would express the same opinion: force over and above that which is necessary is excessive. The officer who uses excessive force must realize the consequences of that action, and will be held accountable. Excessive force is not and will never be authorized under any circumstances.

The following information is provided to assist the officer in dealing with this difficult issue. This information is not intended to answer all questions that could arise. Remember, the officer should follow the guidelines that are established by the security agency. The following are recommendations that may help the officer understand the concepts behind the use of force:

1. The officer should never use force that exceeds that which is necessary.
2. The officer should use only that force necessary to overcome actual resistance, not perceived resistance.
3. Use of lethal force is never authorized in other than extreme life threatening situations. Lethal force is not necessary in any crime involving property thefts.
4. The officer should take every possible opportunity to use means other than force to gain compliance. Any form of force should be the last resort.
5. Negotiation and nonforce resolution to problems is much better than utilization of force. It takes little ability to apply force, but it does take a competent security officer to employ other measures.
6. The officer who uses any form of force should notify his/her supervisor immediately. A complete report of the incident and force used should be documented as soon as possible.
7. Never carry unauthorized weapons. If the officer is not licensed to carry firearms, then firearms should never be carried. Saps or billyclubs should never be authorized equipment. These weapons are considered offensive and can inflict deadly force.
8. Never use equipment as a weapon unless designed for that purpose. A flashlight is not a club and should not be used as one.
9. The officer should never use any weapon as a form of intimidation.
10. If force is used and any form of injury results, the officer must obtain medical assistance for the person injured.
11. The officer must take precautions to avoid injury to any innocent bystander. The officer will be responsible for injury to anyone including the suspect.

12. The officer who uses any force, including restraint holds, must make sure that training and practice with these weapons and techniques is accomplished on a regular basis.

13. The officer should never attempt to use any weapon or restraint procedure he/she is not thoroughly familiar with. The officer who had never used a semi-automatic weapon should not use the weapon until training in its use and safety has been completed. The use of restraint holds that are improperly applied can result in death or serious injury. The officer should never attempt to use restraint techniques that he/she has not been thoroughly trained in, and practiced under professional supervision.

14. The officer should be just as familiar with techniques in verbal conflict resolution as he/she is in the use of force. In fact, the officer should be even more familiar with techniques to reduce conflict by means other than the application of force.

15. The use of force should always be in defense, not aggression. Weapons and restraint techniques should be for defending the officer or citizen, not as instruments of attack.

CHAPTER NINE

Field Contacts

Field Contacts

The job of security officer is one that deals with people. This is a consistent part of the job and should be expected. The officer will encounter all forms of situations, some being positive and some negative. Rarely will the officer have difficulty performing an assignment that has a limited contact with people. The officer who has a high citizen contact assignment will encounter the most difficulty. This situation is not unique to the security field, but is a part of any job that is people oriented. Why this problem exists is a subject for a book that would take days to read. The social aspects of dealing with people are well beyond the scope of this book and would undoubtedly be very philosophical.

However, the following are some general opinions with regard to dealing with the public: One of the first things to consider about field contact with the public is that very few people like being told what to do, or how to do it. There seems to be a natural resentment of anyone representing a form of authority. This resentment becomes even more exaggerated when the authority is being directed toward them. Alcohol related contacts can be the most hostile. This is based on the fact that the person's judgment is altered, and liquid courage is present. People who are drunk, or even slightly under the influence of alcohol, are difficult to control or gain complaince from. People who consider themselves above authority may not become hostile, but can certainly become argumentative and cause a scene or disturbance. People with higher educations seem to be easier to explain things to, but frequently display an above-the-law attitude. Those who are actually violating the law can use many tactics to avoid apprehension and arrest. They will cause scenes and make wild accusations to direct attention away from the fact that they are guilty of a crime or activity. These individuals can also become hostile as time goes on, when their arguments are seen to be of no avail. Remember, these general statements are just that; general opinions that may or may not apply to the individuals being contacted. Although it does justify a need for the officer to be aware of some potential problems that people can present. Do not take the initial conduct of a person as a true display of his/her character or future conduct. To phrase it in a different way, people who display a passive demeanor when initially contacted can become hostile if they feel this conduct will help them to escape or avoid apprehension. This is not always the case but can occur often enough to make the officer wary since he/she is unsure of the actual intentions of the person being contacted.

The officer who contacts a person displaying an immediate hostile attitude or demeanor doesn't have much difficulty figuring out how to handle the situation. It is the person who is erratic in behavior that presents the greatest challenge to officer safety. This concept needs further discussion in order to foster a better understanding. The hostile person would not be approached in the same manner as one who displays no hostility. The officer would take measures to control the hostile person immediately. The person who appears calm and mild mannered will have the advantage of turning hostile without the officer's foreknowledge, or advanced preparation. The officer will usually be rather close to this person, conducting an interview or completing a field contact card. This closeness places the officer at an obvious disadvantage. The hostile person wouldn't have the same advantage, as there is little doubt as to the need for defensive action on the part of the officer.

The uncertainty of the outcome of any field contact requires the officer to develop a routine approach to all contacts. This will permit the officer to respond to any change in attitude or level of hostility. This style is not easy to accomplish, nor is it effective with all situations. The officer who takes particular care not to be too vulnerable will be the one who is prepared for the majority of situations. No one can prepare for every possible situation that could occur. Consequently, it becomes necessary to prepare for the ultimate, yet not to the point of being viewed as aggressive or overbearing. The officer who remembers to keep at least one-arms distance from the person being contacted, does not turn away from that person, if armed, does not turn the weapon towards the person being interviewed, keeps the interview calm and without fluctuations in temperament, and treats everyone in a professional manner will be the officer who is the most prepared. Remember, there is a fine line between acceptable demeanor in citizen contacts and unacceptable conduct. One example would be the officer who always places his hand on his weapon when talking to citizens. This will result in so many complaints of overreaction on the officer's part, that it isn't worth employing this form of behavior. The officer in this case could have accomplished the same effect if he would have his hand close to the weapon, not actually on the weapon.

One of the most routine questions asked about field contacts is regarding how to handle the initial contact. The officer will set the tone for the entire contact by what is said in the first few seconds. The circumstances will dictate the best thing to say, but some general statements can give the officer a basis to begin with. It is recommended that the officer make a simple greeting as the opening comment. An example would be: The officer approaches the person(s) being contacted and says, "Good evening, I am Security Officer Jones. I am the officer who is responsible for the security of this complex. This is a restricted area and I would appreciate it if you would assist us by remaining in the public access area." This opening statement is friendly yet advises the person that he is requested to leave the area. The next statement could consist of the officer thanking the person for complying with the request. It is not necessary to make the request a command to gain compliance. Should the person refuse to comply, the officer may have to insist the person leave. The officer has at least presented his request in a professional manner. It would be difficult for the person to take this form of request in a negative manner. Being polite in no way makes the officer less effective; in fact, it shows that the officer is capable of soliciting compliance without the need for aggressive acts, or a show of authority.

Contact with youths can best be handled with a firm, yet friendly approach. Youths can become very argumentative, but will frequently stop prior to involvement in anything that amounts to a criminal act. The use of parental control should not be ruled out. It may be necessary for the officer to solicit parental intervention if the problem can best be resolved in that fashion. This tactic may not be available to the officer at that immediate moment. The officer may need to meet with the parents at a time after the contact or incident has occurred. Remember, the officer will have to be rather specific when notification of parents is accomplished. They will either support your request; or like some parents will pay little attention based on the fact that their children can do no wrong. This may sound negative, but the reality is that some parents will not believe their child could be involved in any activity that would be considered unacceptable. The officer has made an attempt to resolve the issue in a reasonable manner, and should be commended for the attempt.

With any field contact, the officer should make a note in his/her field notebook, or complete a field contact card so that a record of the incident can be documented. This process will permit the officer to have a file on the person being contacted, which may prove valuable on any future encounters. The person who denies any prior contacts with the officer or another officer will be surprised to find that a file showing the initial contact is available to disprove these statements. This record can also be of value should any event result in an arrest or prosecution. Past contacts with the subject will assist in showing intent or similiar activities.

Reference has been made to field contact cards several times. A field contact card is in reality any form of document that records the contact, and provides a narrative of the circumstances. Many officers will find a preprinted card, which requires only filling in the spaces, the best field contact form to use. These cards can be made up by the officer or printed on agency forms. It does not matter what form is used, as long as the form contains sufficient information to permit anyone to understand what occurred, and a description of the subject contacted. This card should not be so difficult to fill out that there will be an aversion to using it. It can be a valuable tool not only in recording information, but by letting the subject know that a record of the contact has been made. This can prevent the subject from returning to the area and causing any additional problems. This alone makes the field contact card a deterrent.

Senior citizens present a different set of circumstances for the officer. Many senior citizens have physical limitations that may prevent them from understanding the officer's request or directions. Senior citizens should be given special considerations when being contacted. They may become excited and will need special treatment. Remember, the senior citizen is not the usual person being contacted. They seldom present any problem, and are usually the greatest supporters of the police and security officer. Have a little consideration for them by being patient, and assisting them instead of directing them.

CHAPTER TEN

Security Industry-Law Enforcement Partnership

Security Industry-
Law Enforcement
Partnership

The traditional separation between private security and law enforcement is narrowing to the point that a new spirit of cooperation is emerging. The police and security are beginning to see each other as partners in the public safety field. The need to combine efforts is evident by the rising crime rates that affect all levels of society. When the goals and objectives of two organizations are basically indentical, that being to protect and serve, it makes sense to join forces so that these objectives can be achieved.

Change in both attitude and cooperation is not easy to accomplish. It will take a steady progression of trust and understanding on both sides, before an effective working relationship will become reality. One of the first steps to be considered is an increase in the level of communication presently existing. It is an excellent idea for the field officers to communicate with each other, but it is also necessary that management and supervision of both agencies develop lines of communication. Through the exchange of information and concerns, a working relationship can develop that has more than a cordial meaning. This liaison can expand the abilities of both agencies to combat criminal activity which both agree is their primary function.

A partnership cannot exist and thrive if the partnership is dictated. When someone is told, "You will cooperate", it automatically is viewed upon by some with resentment. What has to take place is a mutual desire by both agencies to develop and implement a good working relationship. A partnership based on mutual benefits, that each may receive, is much better than one based on forced participation. To expect anything less would result in a system rather than a partnership. Communication and cooperation would take place, but not on the same level of effectiveness as it would if based on one agency being willing to assist the other.

Someone has to take the initiative to make a partnership a reality. It cannot be just an expression of the desire for a better relationship. There must be a concrete proposal for a coalition to be formed between the security agency and police department. It is just possible that cooperation is already of interest, but some form of catalyst is needed to get the process in motion. It is similar to a person who always had in mind a desire to accomplish something, but never took the first step towards making it a reality. An official proposal to form a partnership, that allows both agencies to perform their job in a more competent manner, is difficult to refuse. It may be discovered that cooperation is easier to accomplish than previously thought possible.

A partnership is only as strong as both parties allow it to be. It takes all members of each organization to function together in order to make a partnership effective. Cooperation cannot be implied, but must be an actual policy that exists. When either party does not take into consideration the interests and concerns of the other, especially in decision-making and policy development, a true partnership is not in existence. It takes every level of authority within both agencies, working as a team, to make this partnership one that is beneficial to the citizens who rely on both police and private security for protection services.

A partnership of this type is not impossible but does take effort and special consideration by all parties to be effective. Remember, some people don't accept change as readily as others, and all resistance will not be overcome overnight. It will take management's support and salesmanship on both agencies to foster acceptance. It may be that some form of relationship and cooperation has been possible in the past, but for unknown reasons did not develop adequately. What is important is the continued progress towards a relationship that will be of benefit to the security industry, the police and the public. It is for this ultimate goal that every avenue should be approached in order to make this partnership become a reality.

CHAPTER ELEVEN

Effective Communications

Effective
Communications

The ability to effectively communicate with others is of such vital importance to the officer's future growth and development that special attention to this subject is necessary. The officer who can speak in a clear and concise manner has the advantage of not needing to repeat information, or have that information misunderstood. What is even more important is the impact on the officer who cannot effectively communicate. This officer will find that the inability to communicate properly can restrict his/her job performance.

It isn't necessary for the officer to be college educated in the fine points of English diction. It is necessary for the officer to have the ability to use the proper wording in order to make his/her statements understood. Everyone, at one time or other, has spoken to an individual who does not have the ability to express his/her ideas and concepts in a clear and concise manner. This person is difficult to listen to, and the true meaning of what is being said gets lost in the translation. It is one thing to say to a person, "I want to see your identification". This is a simple and clear statement. It is difficult for a person to misunderstand what is being requested. However, the statement. "Got anything with your face on it?" could obviously be subject to misunderstanding.

The officer must think before speaking. If a specific request is being made of someone, that person should not have to guess at what is being requested. This concept has little impact on routine requests or conversation, but is of great importance when an emergency is occurring, and concise statements must be used.

This is not the time for confusion or misunderstanding. The officer should be direct and to the point. He/she should not cloud the conversation with statements that are unnecessary and do not relate to the request. The officer who uses short statements has the best opportunity to eliminate confusion.

Concise statements can also make the officer's request for compliance easier to understand. If the officer contacts a person who is in a restricted area and makes the statement, "This is a restricted area, and we are requesting that you remain on public property", little room is left for a misunderstanding of what is being requested. If the officer said to this person, "Hey, I don't think it is a good idea to be here", the officer neglected to say the area is restricted, he/she did not request the person to leave and he/she did not make it clear that the person was on private property. Should the person fail to comply due to a misunderstanding of what was requested, who is at fault?

There are some well educated people who do not know how to speak. There are less educated people who have little difficulty in making themselves understood. These people do not need the use of long sophisticated words, which most people don't understand anyway, in order to have an effective level of communication skills. In fact, many people take offense at someone using unfamiliar terms, and interpret it as an attempt to talk down to them. This permits anger to get in the way of understanding.

The goals to be achieved by the officer concern: obtaining compliance with rules and regulations, gaining information, directing and controlling conduct and fostering positive customer relations. These goals are best accomplished by effective communication skills. The ability to communicate in a friendly, yet firm manner is an indication of the officer's maturity level. The officer who uses street terms, when talking to juveniles or young adults, may find this form of communication acceptable for that age group. However, it would be unwise to communicate in the same manner with adults or senior citizens. It is not acceptable conduct and there is the possibility of complaints against the officer's demeanor.

The officer should take appropriate steps to correct communication problems. Community colleges and adult education centers offer programs in English and oral communication skills. These programs are very effective in teaching proper word usage, as well as public speaking techniques. These programs are inexpensive, and an excellent resource the officer should consider. Another way of developing communication skills is to listen to other officers who do possess these skills. The simple process of listening can enable the officer to pick up on word usage, and proper sentence structure. One of the best advantages realized, while listening to and observing other officers, is the fact that they are usually conducting security business, and therefore, using language relating to it. This language usage in the business setting can differ from social usage. In listening and observing, the officer can realize first hand the proper business use versus the social usage of conversation.

Regardless of the method used to correct communication difficulties, the important fact is that some action should be taken. It will make a tremendous difference in the officer's ability to perform the job as a competent and professional security officer.

CHAPTER TWELVE

Accountability

Accountability

Every employee assumes certain responsibilities when performing job assignments. This fact makes the employee accountable for his/her actions, and the employee will be subject to santions for failure to meet the job specifications. This process is usually accomplished by supervision of the employee's on-the-job performance. This evaluation serves as an indicator of the employee's ability to meet the job demands according to policy and procedure mandates. It is important to remember that whatever the employee does while on the job can be considered as job related. This means that employees who make decisions, that are not in conformance with job regulations, are subject to sanctions and a poor performance rating. The officer who makes too many unacceptable decisions will soon become very hard pressed to justify the employer's contining his/her employment. Thus, it is mandatory that the employee be aware of the fact that actions and conduct on his/her part are subject to accountability and justification.

The employee who assumes that is supervision's responsibility to ensure that he/she performs the job to their specifications may be in for a big surprise. It is supervision's responsibility to ensure that the officer is aware of the job demands, and to train the officer to meet these demands. It is not the role of supervision, however, to stand over the officer to make sure that these demands are being complied with, and that the job is being performed to the appropriate standards. The supervisor, at that point, is supposed to be a resource for the officer, the supervisor should be available to answer questions that relate to the job. If the supervisor must be required to remain at all times with the officer, then why not have the supervisor perform the assignment instead, and save the cost of having the officer on the payroll? So you see, supervision must be a trainer and support for the field officer. Supervision does not have to play the role of baby-sitter in order to get the officer to perform the job.

The officer who makes occasional mistakes is probably doing a good job but, as with everyone, will not always make the right decision. This form of conduct goes along with performing the job, and is expected by every employer. The officer who does little will probably make limited mistakes. The officer who makes errors in judgement, but who sincerely was trying to do a good job, should not be evaluated the same as an officer who does nothing short of the minimal acceptable standards. Certainly, officers should be held accountable for their mistakes, but with reason and understanding. The employee who works hard, and continues to perform a good job, will be the one who receives the most outstanding evaluation. The officer who does little can only expect the evaluation to reflect that the officer deserves improvement-needed ratings.

The following are two main points which must be considered by the officer: First, in order to continue employment, the officer must perform the job in an acceptable manner. Second, the officer will be held accountable for his/her actions while performing the job. The officer who fails to consider the concept of accountability will find supervision difficult to accept. This officer must understand that the role of the organization is to provide a service in the most competent manner possible. Consequently, this requires that every employee direct his/her energy toward accomplishing this goal. The officer who fails to meet these standards will be outside the main focus of the organization. This employee is of little value to the organization, and will not be an employee for long.

The officer who is aware that he/she will be held accountable for his/her actions will act in a manner that does not violate agency rules and regulations. This officer is one who is most valued by the organization. Remember, problem employees require additional supervision that could otherwise be utilized elsewhere for other assignments. Why would an agency continue to employ someone who fails to meet the standards of conduct and job performance? They will not, and should not. It is in the officer's best interest to keep this concept in mind at all times. Remembering this will prevent unnecessary discipline, up to and including termination, from having to be levied against the officer. A problem employee on one job will have a difficult time in obtaining employment on another job. No agency wants to hire an employee who refuses to be accountable for his/her actions and job performance.

CHAPTER THIRTEEN

Officer Safety Considerations

Officer Safety Considerations

The officer who accepts the job of a security officer, also must accept the fact that the job requires being involved in situations which can be hazardous. The following presentation of officer safety considerations is not intended to be a complete list of all officer safety concepts or subjects which the officer must be knowledgeable about. The following list is for the officer's consideration and incorporation into his/her personal style of performance:

1. The officer should always consider the persons contacted may present a possible situation that could be potentially hazardous. They can inflict bodily harm to the officer, if the opportunity presents itself. The officer should not allow an opportunity for anyone to catch him/her off guard. The officer must be alert, but at the same time not allow officer safety concerns to prevent him/her from doing the assigned job.

2. The officer should never work when fatigue prevents his/her from being fully awake and aware of the surroundings. When the officer is in this condition, he/she should not be permitted to work on field assignments.

3. The officer should never confront hostile persons alone. The police or additional officers should be requested, and be present on the scene, before any hostile person is contacted or apprehended.

4. The officer should always be in good physical condition. To attempt to perform a job that is not physically possible is unsafe and not recommended.

5. The safety equipment worn by the officer should at all times be in proper working order. Weapons should be clean and free from any mechanical defects. Batons should be worn in the proper way and should be made only of authorized materials. Chemical mace should show an effective expiration date, and any expired canisters should be destroyed and replaced with new materials.

6. The officer should never allow courage to overshadow good judgement. The officer who enters areas that are potential hazards, without proper precautionary measures being applied, is not using good judgement. The officer is foolish if he/she feels that there is no need for assistance in hazardous situations. At one time or another, he/she will find this to be an unsafe decision. There is always someone out there who is willing and capable of inflicting injury to the officer if he/she is caught unprepared, no matter how fit the officer appears.

7. The officer should never approach a group of people without first requesting the proper backup, even though it may not be needed. The officer will have to take the circumstances into consideration, and determine if the situation warrants additional assistance. Remember, calling wolf will result in the same response, as not calling at all. The assistance may not arrive, or may take too much time in responding.

8. The officer should never walk directly in front of the vehicle headlights when approaching an occupied vehicle. This illuminates the officer and allows anyone inside the vehicle to know the exact position of the officer.

9. When using a flashlight, the officer should never hold the light next to his/her body. This procedure would permit the officer's actual location to be known. It is recommended that the flashlight be held away from the body, at arms length. This will prevent the officer's position from being known.

10. The officer should make a habit of looking around corners of buildings before making his presence known. This pro-

cedure will allow the officer to know what is around the corner prior to making an entry into the area.

11. It is recommended that any item being carried by the officer should be secured to prevent any unnecessary noise from being generated. Keys, batons or any other equipment should not be allowed to make noise that would give the officer's location away.

12. The officer should cover up badges or any other reflective objects that would allow the officer's location to be known. At night these items reflect available light and will show the officer's position. Cover these items up until they are necessary.

13. The officer should never have the unit radio or portable radio on so loud that the officer's ability to remain undetected is compromised. Keep these radios low enough to still permit reception, yet not so loud that they create a hazard.

14. The officer should know his/her exact location at all times. In the event the need for assistance arises, the officer needs to promptly relay this information or it can prevent assistance from arriving in time.

15. The officer should never be so far away from his/her vehicle, or any form of communication, that he/she would be prevented from obtaining assistance. The officer who parks the vehicle, and conducts foot patrol that takes him/her a long distance away from the vehicle, will not have the ability to exit the area rapidly if the need arises.

16. The officer should never have a weapon drawn as a tactic to scare someone or intimidate them. The potential of the weapon being taken away from the officer and being used against him/her poses a real danger.

17. The officer should never take aggressive action against anyone. Officers should only react in defense of themselves, other citizens or the extreme potential of violence.

18. The officer should expect the unexpected to happen. This is not to suggest that the officer needs to maintain a constant, heightened sense of awareness, but only serves to reinforce the officer's understanding that the unexpected

can occur, and not to allow him/herself to be taken by surprise.

19. The officer should maintain a constant communication process with the dispatcher or other officers working the field. This will allow for assistance, and potential problems to be communicated without delay.

20. The officer should be aware of the fact that family disturbances present the greatest potential for injury. The officer who confronts even the smallest family disturbance should not make contact without backup assistance being present. This rule should never be violated.

21. The officer should never permit him/herself to carry anything in the hand that would be used to draw or use a weapon. Get into the habit of always keeping that hand free.

22. The officer should never work with a partner that has been drinking, or that has used any form of narcotic. This places both officers in a potentially hazardous situation, and this should not be tolerated. This person needs to be removed from the work environment, and should not be allowed to return without undergoing some form of treatment or rehabilitation.

23. The officer who finds an unsafe condition on the job site should make sure that condition is corrected. The hazard that is allowed to remain can be the condition that causes the officer to be injured at a later date.

24. The officer who cannot perform the job in a competent and safe manner would be foolish if he/she didn't request an assignment that is within his/her abilities. This may be difficult for the officer to admit, but it certainly is the safest way to address the issue. An example would be an officer who has a physical limitation which prohibits rapid movement. This limitation would also prevent the officer from being able to physically protect him/herself. The officer should take an assignment that would not pose any potential hazards.

25. The officer should never allow personal problems to come to the job. Everyone has some problem of a personal nature at one time or another. Officers must avoid allowing these

problems to influence their abilities and the performance of their job. Officers must be free to do their job in a safe and conscientious manner. Personal problems must be kept off the job. If this is not done, the problem can prevent awareness and get in the way of good judgement.

26. Stress is as much of a problem on the job as off. The officer who is experiencing stress symptoms should take appropriate steps to reduce the stress level by medical or other means. The officer will find that stress can make the job impossible to perform, and can result in some severe disability problems.

27. The officer should make sure that all of the equipment needed to do the job is available for use. The officer who is on night patrol without a flashlight might be hard pressed to locate one when it is required immediately. It may not be possible to halt activity so that the officer can locate his equipment. Remember to check your equipment and make sure it works properly before needing it, not at the time it could pose an officer safety problems.

28. The officer should utilize some form of physical fitness program in order to keep in shape. The benefits derived from physical fitness not only prevent medical problems that come with inactivity, but also keep the officer in condition. A physically fit officer can overcome the potential for physical harm that could result from an altercation with a suspect.

29. The officer should never permit his weapon or baton to be accessible to any suspect, or person being interviewed. Keep these weapons as far away from the suspect's reach as possible!

30. The officer should always keep an eye on every person being contacted. The officer must not allow one subject to distract his/her attention, while other subjects are present.

31. The officer should make sure that all subjects being contacted remain in front of the officer. It is unsafe to allow subjects to walk around, especially behind the officer.

32. The officer should remain calm at all times during contacts with subjects. The officer's demeanor will dictate the attitude and response some subjects will focus on. The officer

who can maintain a composure that is nonaggressive and nonreactive will keep the situation from escalating. The officer should remember that some subjects will attempt to get the officer angry or nervous, for no better reason then to make the officer lose control.

33. The officer should never allow comfort to get in the way of safety. Wearing excessive and bulky clothing that does not permit easy access to emergency equipment, weapons, baton or the radio is putting him/herself in a very awkward position, as well as a hazardous situation.

34. The officer who puts safety above job performance will not be effective. The officer who puts the job above safety, also will not be effective. The officer must develop a balance between both concerns, in order to be effective in both areas.

CHAPTER FOURTEEN

Conflict Resolution

Conflict
Resolution

The ability to resolve conflict by means of verbal persuasion is a talent that many people do not possess. The average person does not take the time to handle conflict by means other than aggressive verbal or physical behavior. The person who seldom comes into contact with hostile or abusive situations may not consider conflict resolution as an alternative. They frequently remove themselves from the situation with the least amount of embarrassment possible. This response is very effective for this person, but the security officer cannot simply turn around and allow the issue to go unresolved. The security officer in most cases will not resolve the issue by avoidance, but must develop some form of acceptable solution. The security officer who fails to resolve the issue may encounter the same situation over and over again.

The officer should understand that a hostile situation is separate from combative situations. In this context, hostile situations are those that involve contacts with persons who are angry, upset or argumentative. The combative situation is one where physical force of some type is necessary to prevent officer injury or overcome resistance. Hostile situations can result in combative situations depending on how they are handled. A combative situation can be calmed if the officer can develop a technique of conflict resolution by means of verbal persuasion.

No concrete techniques exist that will guarantee a successful solution to conflict problems. The calm, understanding approach to reduce hostility may work with some individuals, but not with others. Rigid demands and orders directed at some individuals may not reduce hostility, but escalate the situation. The officer should develop a standard method of conflict resolution, while realizing that modifications may be necessary.

One approach to reduce hostility is to remain calm with no outward display of emotion. The officer should listen to the hostile person's complaint or story without interjecting comments or opinions. Once the person has completed the story, the officer should repeat the main points surrounding the complaint. This can be accomplished with a statement such as "You feel that", then repeat the most important points back to the individual. This tactic shows the person that you were listening, that you are interested in their problem, and allows the hostile person to calm down while the officer is talking. The officer should then advise the person what he/she can do to assist. The statement, "I can help you with most of your concerns but I may not be able to satisfy your entire problem", is effective if the officer can help with some parts of the complaint, but not every point. The immediate follow-up statement should be, "Let's take care of those things I can help with, then I will direct you to the person who may be able to assist you with the other issues". This statement makes it very difficult for the person to refuse your assistance. When a person feels they are being helped, their hostility can be greatly reduced. The officer must make sure he/she can help the person before offering any assistance. False promises can make the problem even more difficult, when the person realized the officer was not truthful. Once the officer has rendered the assistance that he/she can provide, it is important to follow through by directing the person to the individual who can continue resolving the problem.

If at all possible, never leave a hostile situation unresolved, or at least attempt to reduce the tension level. A possibility of what can happen is the transfer of a hostile situation to another officer, who may be less sensitive to conflict resolution. Remember, a person who undergoes a continuous process of being put off does not become less aggressive, but usually shows an increase in hostility. The next officer who comes in contact with this person may have to take physical action to prevent injury to him/herself or innocent victims. Unresolved hostility remains a hazardous situation not only for the officer, but also for others who may come in contact with this angry person.

The security officer needs to be constantly aware of any form of body language that would give the impression that he/she is about to use aggressive action. A combative stance is one of the most direct forms of body language that depicts the officer's willingness to use force in order to resolve the problem. Even if this is not the intended response, the hostile person can perceive this as a challenge. The officer should remain in a posture that allows response to combative attack, but not ask for it. The officer does not have to keep his/her hands on weapons in order to respond to aggressive acts. This is the most direct display of the officer's intention to respond with force. The officer can accomplish the same precautionary techniques by observing the suspect's actions and by paying special attention to any sudden elevation in emotional behavior. Remember, anyone can strike out without warning. This may be impossible to predict or prepare for by using defensive action. Generally, a process of escalation is seen before any combative action is taken. The officer, who is aware of this process, can take action to calm the subject before the situation reaches the combative stage. Some of the indications of the process the officer should look for are: signs of increased agitation in the subject's voice or body movements, rapid increase in speech, taking a combative stance, facial expressions which show that anger is increasing and conversation that turns into yelling. These are not the only indicators of a person who may become combative, but represent some obvious signs to be aware of. Once these signs become evident, the officer should make every attempt to reduce tension and anxiety.

Hostility can be reduced in several ways. For example, the officer can ask the person to calm down, so that a rational discussion can take place. One technique that has proven successful is to tell the person, "I am here to help you, but unless you calm down, nothing can be done about your problem." The officer can also say, "How can you expect anyone to help you unless you let them?" "I can't help you until we can discuss the problem in a reasonable manner." What is said to the hostile person must be presented in a calm and reassuring manner. The person does not necessarily need assurance that the officer is on his/her side, but the person does not want to feel that the officer is against him/her either. The neutral approach is the best way to address the subject's problem.

Hostility that is directed toward the officer due to demands he/she has made on the subject is different from hostility that is generated by someone else's actions or conduct. The officer who advises a person that their presence or activity is unauthorized, and is met with hostility, may have to approach this situation in a different manner. The person who shows resistance to the officer's demands may not respond to any form of reasoning. The officer may have to resort to the simple tactic of advising the subject that his/her compliance is requested, and that a confrontation is not the officer's objective. If the subject does not comply, the officer should not continue a lengthy debate. This usually accomplishes little in the way of problem resolution. The officer should advise the subject that if the activity is not stopped, he/she will be subject to additional action. If this direct statement does not resolve the problem, the officer should not continue making requests for complaince. If the situation is a violation of the law, the officer can make a citizen's arrest, or request the local police to respond for the arrest or removal of the subject. Caution should be used in this situation. Remember, the officer should never become involved in a potential hostile situation without proper backup. The police should be requested, as soon as it becomes apparent that compliance is not going to be accomplished without other action being taken on the part of the officer.

The officer should never use threats as a tactic to obtain compliance. It doesn't take long for the subject to realize that this tactic is being used, and as a result the person may continue to resist the officer's demands. If the situation is such that official action is needed, then the officer may have to use this approach to resolve the problem. Nothing is accomplished by a problem remaining unresolved. The officer may have to address the same situation at a later date, along with the potential for an escalated confrontation. Use the tactic of requesting compliance until this tactic is no longer effective. The use of forced compliance should be the last resort, but the officer should use this form of action if no other means is available.

Conflict resolution is not easy to accomplish. The security officer is being confronted with hostility that he/she probably knows little about. The officer, however, is being relied upon to resolve it. Success or failure to resolve conflict depends on the officer's own level of maturity and his/her willingness to develop the "people skills" necessary to communicate in adverse situations. Once the officer has developed these skills, his/her value as a security professional has increased dramatically.

CHAPTER FIFTEEN

*Arrest and Control
Techniques*

Arrest and Control Techniques

The security officer will encounter situations that require the physical arrest and control of suspected criminals. The process of taking someone into custody is one of the most hazardous situations an officer can encounter. The most important factor to be taken into consideration is the suspect's reaction to being arrested, which can never be absolutely known. A suspect who is calm during the initial contact, can immediately become combative when faced with arrest. A combative response may not always be the suspect's reaction, but it does occur with a very high rate of frequency.

The officer who is prepared for a hostile reaction can overcome potential resistance by using common sense and a professional demeanor. These two approaches can prevent the suspect from taking advantage of the officer. It is important to remember that suspects, when confronted with an arrest situation, may resist if they feel the officer does not have the knowledge and experience to handle the arrest. Suspects are not stupid. They can detect an inexperienced officer almost immediately. Suspects who feel that they can avoid arrest by resistance will certainly attempt to do so with an officer they perceive as lacking the ability to control the situation.

Several techniques exist that allow the officer to safely arrest and control a suspect. Some techniques are used in high risk situations, while other techniques are suited for less hazardous conditions. Remember, the proper technique to use in a given situation depends on several factors, such as the suspect's emotional state, physical surroundings, nature of the offense and the potential for weapons to be concealed on the suspect. All of these factors, and many more, have to be considered by the officer who is making the actual arrest. The officer will also find that variations of techniques can be used, which would depend upon the officer's preference.

The following arrest and control techniques are only a few of the procedures being taught. Variations and the mixing of techniques is not uncommon. The officer should realize that any recommended technique should be practiced and thoroughly understood before being applied.

Interrogation Stance

1. Stand with one foot positioned in front of the other, similar to a boxing stance.
2. Place 60% of your body weight on the rear foot, with 40% of body weight on the front foot. The 60/40 stance allows proper balance for easy movement from front to rear.
3. Bend the knees slightly to avoid a rigid stance.

Pat Down Search and Handcuffing Technique

1. From a safe distance, at least five feet, the officer should advise the suspect that a search for weapons is going to be conducted.
2. Make sure the suspect understands what you want him to do. Take charge, but don't be offensive.
3. Tell the suspect to raise his hands and lock his elbows.
4. Tell the suspect to turn slowly to his right and keep turning until told to stop.
5. Stop the suspect when he is facing away from you.
6. Tell the suspect to place his left hand in the small of his back, then place the right hand in the same position. Then tell him to put his knuckles together. Once this is accomplished, tell him to interlace his fingers.
7. Tell the suspect to spread his legs and point his toes outward.
8. Once the suspect is in this position, the last thing to tell him is not to move from this position.

9. As you approach the suspect from the rear, tell him to turn his head to the right and look down. This cuts down his field of vision.

10. Approach the suspect from his left side, keeping your gun side away from him.

11. Grasp the top four fingers of the suspect's hand with your right hand, and the remaining fingers with your left hand. If need be, you may have to regrip the suspect's fingers to maintain good control.

12. Release your left hand and proceed to search the left side of the suspect , including his leg area. Your left foot should be inside of the suspect's left foot, at his ankle.

13. Search methodically, checking for weapons starting with the head, moving down to his ankles.

14. Still holding on with your right hand, slowly slide your left hand into place, as you replace your right hand with your left hand. Your left hand should now be the controlling hand.

15. Move your left foot so it is against the suspect's right ankle. Repeat the same search techniques on the right side.

16. If the suspect is going to be released after the pat down search, tell him you are going to release him, and that you want him to follow your instructions. Tell him to take two steps forward, then he can turn around and face you.

Handcuffing From Pat Down Search

The officer should understand that any suspect can be handcuffed prior to any search being conducted. It is not necessary to search a suspect before handcuffing if that person is going to be arrested anyway. It is much safer to handcuff the person before any search is conducted. If, during the search a non-handcuffed person, the officer finds a weapon or contraband, the officer can handcuff the suspect from the pat down position by the following process:

1. Without releasing the suspect's hands with your left hand, take out your cuffs with your right hand, and hold them so you are looking at the keyholes.

2. Grasping the cuffs firmly, turn the cuffs downward, cuffing the suspect's right hand first.
3. With the cuffs still in your grip, pull the cuffs toward the suspect's left hand and push them downward, cuffing his left hand.
4. Once the suspect is handcuffed, then a complete search can be conducted in a safe manner.

Kneeling Search and Cuffing Technique

The kneeling search and cuffing techniques provide the officer more safety than a standing search and cuffing position. The officer can accomplish this technique by using the following procedures:

1. From a safe distance, at least five feet away, advise the suspect to turn to his right until told to stop.
2. Stop the suspect when he is facing away from you. The suspect should have his back turned toward you.
3. Tell the suspect to place his hands on top of his head and interlace his fingers.
4. Tell the suspect to drop down to his knees, keeping his hands on his head.
5. Tell the suspect to cross his legs at the ankles and remain in that position.
6. Order the suspect to look to the right and lower his head. Advise the suspect to remain in that position and not to move.
7. Approach the suspect from the left side and grab the suspect's first four fingers with your right hand, pulling them back toward you. This will pull the suspect's torso backwards, causing him to be off balance.
8. If a search is to be conducted, start with the suspect's left side making a complete search. When completed, replace your right hand with your left hand and complete a search of the suspect's right side.
9. If the suspect is going to be handcuffed, hold the suspect's fingers with your left hand and obtain the handcuffs with your right hand. With the keyholes in the upright position,

place the handcuffs on the suspect's right wrist first. Bring the suspect's right arm around to the small of his back, while still holding on to the handcuffs with your right hand. With your left hand, bring the suspect's left arm around to the small of his back. Place the other cuff on the suspect's left hand.

10. Once handcuffed, assist the suspect to his feet and, if necessary, complete a more thorough search of the suspect.
11. If the suspect is not going to be handcuffed, the officer is to tell the suspect to remain in that position until told to move. The officer should then step back a few feet, and tell the suspect to stand up and take two steps forward. Then tell the suspect to turn around and face you.

High Risk Search and Handcuffing Technique

The officer can complete a safe high risk search and handcuffing procedure by taking into consideration the following techniques:

1. Advise the suspect to do exactly what you say.
2. Give orders slowly and with good voice control.
3. Have the suspect turn to his right as you visually check his waistband and the area around his chest for any bulges.
4. Once you have checked him, make sure he is facing you.
5. Order him down to his knees.
6. Have him place his hands out in front of him.
7. Tell him to slide his legs back until flat on the ground.
8. Order him to place his hands out to the side, palms up, like a cross.
9. Have him point his toes out so that the inside of his ankles are against the ground.
10. Order him to turn his head to the left and not to move from that position.
11. Approach the suspect slowly and pick up his right hand.
12. With his arm in a locked position, walk forward and drop your right knee to the suspect's neck and your left knee to the suspect's back.

13. Make sure the suspect's fingers are always pointed toward his head.
14. Reach with your right hand and obtain your handcuffs. Order the suspect to place his left hand on the small of his back and raise his arm in the air.
15. Reach under the suspect's hand, and place the handcuffs on the suspect's left hand.
16. Bring the suspect's right arm down and place the handcuffs on his right hand. Remember, do not release pressure on the suspect's uncuffed hand until it is cuffed.
17. Once cuffed, the officer can standup and assist the suspect to his feet. Have him roll over and sit cross-legged, then stand up on the count of three and assist him as he does it. Don't expect the suspect to be a gymnast. Remember, he is handcuffed, making standing up difficult.

Remember, these arrest and control techniques are only recommendations. The officer must incorporate these techniques into his own personal style of handling these situations. No single technique will be the best in all situations. The officer can modify any technique to suit the situation. Training and experience in the use of arrest and control procedures is the key to the effective use of these techniques. The officer is the actual decision maker when it comes to the proper method to be used in a given situation. The officer should select the technique that offers him/her the safest way to accomplish the job assignment. Officer safety, combined with the officer's ability to perform the job in a competent manner, is the key to a successful conclusion to a potentially hazardous job task.

WEAPONLESS DEFENSE TECHNIQUES

Weaponless defense techniques are designed so that the possibility of injury resulting from confrontation situations involving the security officer can be reduced. As with other techniques, weaponless defense requires training in the use and consequences that may result with application of these tactics. Weaponless defense techniques presented in this guide require physical contact with the suspect in defense situations, not as aggressive acts. The security officer must understand that physical confrontations have the greatest potential for injury to the suspect, or to the officer defending himself. It is of the utmost importance that security officers who use any defensive tactics be trained in the proper use and application techniques. This training should be under professional supervision by defensive tactics instructors who specialize in training others to safely apply these techniques.

Wrist Throw Take Down Technique

The wrist throw down technique is for use when a suspect attempts to grab the officer by the collar, to resist or attack the officer. This technique can be accomplished by using the following procedures:

1. Suspect reaches towards the officer with his right hand, and attempts to grab the officer's collar or shirt.
2. The officer should reach up with his left hand and grab the suspect's right hand at his wrist area.
3. Make sure to place your left thumb at the back of the suspects hand. Reaching around with the fingers of your left hand, grasp the suspect's hand, encircling the thick position of his thumb.
4. Bring your right hand up to assist, placing your right thumb next to your left thumb. Force the suspect's hand off of your collar by snapping your thumbs in a downward motion towards the ground.
5. The suspect's hand should now be turned in an upward position with his palms up. Step backwards to pull the suspect off balance, and take him all the way to the ground. By stepping completely around the suspect's head, this will automatically move him into the high risk position for handcuffing.
6. Handcuff, search, and then pickup the suspect for transportation, or leave the suspect in the prone position until assistance has arrived.

Arm Bar Wrist Lock Take Down Technique

The arm bar wrist lock take down technique is another defensive tactic to be used when a suspect attempts to grab the officer. The application of this technique permits the officer to take the suspect to the ground into the prone handcuffing position. The officer can utilize this technique by following these procedures:

1. The suspect reaches for or tries to grab the officer with his right hand to resist or inflict injury.
2. The officer reaches across with his right hand and grabs the suspect's right hand at the wrist area. The officer's right thumb should be in the back of the suspect's hand.
3. Turn the suspect's hand so that his palm is now turned up.
4. The officer takes his left hand and places it on top of the suspect's right elbow, applying pressure by pushing downward on the suspect's elbow.
5. The officer then forces the suspect to the ground by the application of pressure to the elbow area while taking the suspect to the ground.
6. The suspect is now in the prone position for handcuffing and arrest.

Hip Throw Take Down Technique

The hip throw take down technique is a defensive tactic to be used when the suspect attempts to strike the officer. The hip throw take down is accomplished in the following manner:

1. When the suspect attempts to strike the officer with his right hand, the officer should block the punch with his left forearm extended, and grasp the suspect's arm at his wrist.
2. Stepping forward with your right leg, place your right foot just past the suspect's right foot. This places the suspect's stomach area at your right hip. Your feet should be close to each other at a 45 degree angle.
3. Put your right arm around the suspect's back and pull him close to your body.
4. While pulling on the suspect's right hand, with your left

hand pull the suspect onto your back, and using your hips throw him to the ground.

5. While controlling the suspect's right hand, move into the Arm Bar lock. From this position, the suspect can be handcuffed and placed in a controlled hold.

Shoulder Throw Take Down Technique

The shoulder throw take down technique is another defensive tactic that can prevent injury when the suspect attempts to strike the officer. The following procedure will permit the safe take down of the suspect:

1. When the suspect attempts to strike the officer with his right hand the officer should block the punch with his/her left forearm extended, and grasp the suspect's arm at his wrist, his/her right hand over the top of both of the suspect's hands.
2. The officer should step forward with his/her right leg, turning his/her body so that the suspect's right armpit is now sitting on top of the officer's right shoulder.
3. With the suspect's right hand still in your grasp, turn his hand so that the palm is now facing up. Apply direct pressure to the suspect's elbow with your right hand, keeping it locked, while pushing up slightly with your left hand.
4. Bring your hips square to the front, with your legs close together at 45 degree angles. Keep the knees bent, pull the suspect onto your back as you straighten both of your legs to lift the suspect off the ground.
5. As you pick the suspect up, pull on his left hand at his wrist to assist you in the throw.
6. Once the suspect is up, pull his body over your back and throw him to the ground. The officer still retains control of the suspect's right hand.
7. Once the suspect is on the ground, place the suspect's right hand into the arm bar wrist lock position.
8. The suspect can then be moved into the prone position for the high risk cuffing technique.

ESCAPES

The officer may find situations where he/she is placed in control holds by suspects who are attempting to resist arrest or overpower the officer. The following four escape techniques can help the officer to overcome these holds, and complete a safe arrest without injury to him/herself or the suspect. Remember, as with any control technique, the officer must practice techniques and become proficient in their use. The four escape techniques are as follows:

Headlock Hold

1. When the suspect grabs the officer around the neck to execute a headlock, the officer should reach up with his/her hand and grab the suspect's hair as he/she stomps on the suspect's foot.
2. With the officer's right hand, he/she should grab the suspect's right wrist and pull down on his wrist, so that the officer can establish an airway to breathe.
3. Once the suspect breaks his hold, the officer should retain control of the suspect's right hand, and take the suspect to the ground using an arm bar wrist lock technique.
4. The officer should move the suspect into the prone position for the high risk cuffing and arrest technique.

Bear Hug

1. The officer has various options for obtaining release from the suspect's bear hug hold. Examples of these options follow:
   a. Head butt to the rear, impacting on the suspect's nose.
   b. Foot stomp.
   c. Hammer fist strike to the groin.
   d. Elbow strike to the suspect's ribs.
2. Once the suspect has released his hold, reach over with your left hand and grab the suspect's right wrist. Lock the suspect's right elbow into place on your right shoulder, and pick up the suspect with a shoulder throw.

3. Once the suspect is on the ground, move into the arm bar wrist lock technique. From this position, the suspect can be handcuffed.

Front Choke Hold

1. When the suspect with both hands has grabbed the officer around the neck from the front, the officer should raise his/her right hand over the top of both of the suspect's hands, and pivot sharply to the officer's left. This pivoting will cause the suspect to loosen his grip from around the officer's neck.
2. While pivoting, the officer should raise his/her right foot and back kick the suspect in the groin area with a heel kick.
3. The officer can then take the suspect to the ground with the use of a baton strike, by arm wrist take down techniques or by verbal instructions.

Rear Choke Hold

1. When the suspect has the officer in a rear choke hold, the officer must first obtain breathing clearance. This is done by pulling down on the suspect's forearm and biceps.
2. The officer can then strike the suspect in the groin area with a hammer fist blow, or complete a foot stomp. The use of a shoulder throw may not cause the suspect to release his hold. The officer may have to land backwards on top of the suspect. This may be effective. However, the officer should realize that the results may put him/her in an awkward position, once the suspect releases his hold.
3. Once the suspect has released his hold, the officer should take the ·suspect down into the prone position for handcuffing.

CHAPTER SIXTEEN

*Future of the
Private Security
Industry*

Future of the Private Security Industry

The private security industry is in one of the most advantageous positions in its history. The rising crime rate, combined with the demand for increased security services, makes the private security industry one that will grow at an astronomical rate. The trend to limit the spending of public funds for police services, does not appear to be changing in the immediate future. Police departments are not keeping pace with the population growth, which equates to a reduction of services they are able to provide to the community. When police services are reduced, a void is created that must be filled. The private security industry is the organization that is called upon to offset the services that traditional law enforcement can no longer provide.

However, the growth of the private security industry should not be looked at with total pleasure. Security agencies have some valid concerns that will have to be addressed. Recruitment of qualified personnel, training, supervision and management, capital outlay expenses and the delivery of quality security services are only a few of the concerns the security industry will encounter. Any one of these concerns can effect the security agencies ability to meet the demands being asked of them. The agency that is awarded a large contract, but cannot provide a sufficient level of competent personnel, will soon find itself in a serious situation. This problem can be compounded if the agency has expended a tremendous amount of agency funds for additional equipment and administrative man hours. The corporation that awarded the contract would be under no obligation to retain a security agency that fails to meet contractual requirements.

The issue of qualified personnel appears to be the biggest problem the security agency will face. The employment of officers who are willing to do a good job does not address the problem of training and supervising these employees. As the demand for private security increases, so does the demand for higher levels of performance. Increased performance requires increased training that each officer must receive. Training is an expensive process with no guarantee of a return on the employer's investment. This situation is compounded when expensive training is given employees who do not remain with the agency, or do not meet performance standards.

The security officer will be subject to a higher level of expectation concerning his/her ability to perform a variety of job assignments. One benefit that may result is the requirement for the officer to increase his/her job knowledge. Even if this knowledge increase is forced upon the officer, it will nontheless benefit the agency by having more qualified employees, and also benefit the officer by making him/her a more competent employee.

If predictions come true, private security will begin to assume functions which were traditionally law enforcement responsibilities. If this expansion takes place, the security industry will have to meet even higher performance expectations. Major recruitment and training efforts will be necessary in order to employ the most qualified security staff possible.

It appears that the security industry is in the position to become a vital force in the delivery of public and private security services. If success is to be achieved, the security industry should begin the preparation process now, not when new demands are forced upon them. The entire security profession, security agencies and individual officers as well, will benefit from this advanced planning process.

The security officer should realize that expansion and growth of the security industry can also mean additional opportunities for advancement. While the security industry should plan for future needs, the individual officer should also prepare. He/she should have the vision to seize the opportunity to make themselves the security supervisors and managers of the future.

Increased job knowledge and experience, combined with advanced education achievements, will make the officer a valuable employee.

No one will make the choices for you. It is up to the individual to reach out and achieve whatever goals and objectives they set for themselves. It will take dedication and endurance to accomplish these goals and objectives. But the rewards, in the long run, will far exceed the time and energy expended.

There are no guarantees for success. However, one thing is certain: no one will hand you advancement without first proving yourself capable of handling a management role. Planning and preparation for the future is one investment that is never a waste of time!